Rees, David
　　　Painted desert, green shade

DATE DUE

Painted Desert, Green Shade

Essays on
contemporary writers of
fiction for children and
young adults

by David Rees

The Horn Book Inc
Boston   1984

Printed in the United States of America

Library of Congress Cataloging in Publication Data

Rees, David, 1936-
   Painted desert, green shade.

   Includes bibliographies.
   1. American fiction—20th century—History and criticism. 2. Children's stories, American—History and criticism. 3. English fiction—20th cen-tury—History and criticism. 4. Children's stories, English—History and criticism. I. Title.
PS379.R38   1984   813'.54'099282   83-12996
ISBN 0-87675-286-5

He saw The Last Visible Dog in all the brightness of its lights against the night; he heard the singing and the merriment inside; and he smiled and spoke to the mouse and his child for the second time.

"Be happy," said the tramp.

— Russell Hoban, *The Mouse and His Child*

There's no such thing as fairness. It's a word made up to keep children quiet. When you discover it's a fraud then you're starting to grow up.

— Jan Mark, *Thunder and Lightnings*

For Lee and Robert Natti

Contents

Acknowledgments

Most of this book was written in various different places in California, so my thanks are due to many people in San José, Los Gatos, and San Francisco, particularly Tom Holt and Marian Robinson; to the librarians of Los Gatos Public Library; and to the librarians of California State University, San José.

I would also like to thank Lee Kingman for patience, encouragement, and time.

Four of these essays appeared, in slightly different form, in other publications. Two — on Jan Mark and John Rowe Townsend — were published in *The School Librarian*, in September 1981 and March 1983 respectively; the essay on Robert Westall was published in *Children's Book Bulletin*, Winter 1980, and the essay on Ted Hughes appeared in *San José Studies*, July 1983.

Introduction

"Who can say what is the right book for the right child?"
Bertha Mahony Miller asked in a *Horn Book Magazine* editorial in November 1939. "That, thank God," she said, in
answer to her own question, "is the child's own adventure."
This comment neatly refutes something that is often asked
of authors, critics, teachers and librarians, a question that
irritates them almost more than any other — "What kind
of child is this book for, what age is it aimed at?" — as if a
story were some kind of missile, or capsule full of wise, or
not so wise, precepts, to be hurled at the unsuspecting
young reader's head. The irritation derives from the assumptions behind the question: that a children's book is
not to be regarded in the same way as a novel for adults,
that it cannot be judged solely as a work of art. Barbara
Harrison, in "Why Study Children's Literature?" says —

> It would be foolish to assert that because a book is
> accessible to children or published by a children's de-
> partment of a publishing house, it is less a work of art
> or has less integrity of vision than a book published
> by the general department of the house. It would be
> equally foolish to assert that the blank piece of paper
> is less challenging to the author of a children's book.
> Simplicity or complexity of language has little to do
> with depth of feeling, credibility, or integrity of vi-
> sion.

There are any number of children's books published in the
nineteenth and twentieth centuries that can and should be
judged in exactly the same way that a critic would write
about Tolstoy or Jane Austen. "Acceptability to a child,"
Paul Heins wrote in "Out on a Limb with the Critics," "is a
question concerning book selection and not a fundamental
critical question — not a question of literary criticism."

Margery Fisher says, in *Intent on Reading*, that "to keep
in touch with the likes and dislikes of the young is essen-
tial for any critic of literature," but in this book of thirteen

essays I am, like Paul Heins, not concerned with book selection or acceptability to a child, though I am glad to hear that the novels of, for instance, M.E. Kerr are popular with her young audience, and I regret that much of Virginia Hamilton's work is obscure to many readers of all ages. A major function of criticism is, C. S. Lewis said in *An Experiment in Criticism*, that it "casts a retrospective light on what we have already read. It may sometimes correct an over-emphasis or a neglect in our previous reading and thus improve a future re-reading." This is certainly a purpose I have in mind in these essays — to cast a retrospective light on, for example, the work of Lucy Boston, to correct what I see as an over-emphasis on the value of an author such as Robert Westall, to suggest that in Britain the novels of Jane Langton are unjustly ignored. Roger Rosenblatt in "The Odd Pursuit of Teaching Books" said that a teacher can be a middleman, but "in the best circumstances the middleman becomes a magnifying glass ('Do you see *this*?')." The same remark applies equally well to the critic, or at least to what he hopes he is doing. Critic and teacher have similar, maybe at times the same, functions. Both wish to convey their enthusiasm, and their distaste, for certain works of literature, to impart to others something of their own beliefs, their own morality as it is mirrored in what they read, because literature is, or should be, about life and living. It is of course no substitute for living, but it enhances our experience and our perceptions of others. We are, it is said, what we eat, but we are also undoubtedly what we read.

Painted Desert, Green Shade is not intended to follow exactly the same format as my previous book of essays on contemporary American and British authors of children's and young adult fiction, *The Marble in the Water*. In that first book I was trying to avoid what I regarded, and still regard, as a fault in John Rowe Townsend's *A Sense of Story* — using an inordinate amount of space to summarize the plots of the novels he was discussing. I wanted to cast "a retrospective light on what we have already read." I think now that I sometimes threw the baby out with the bath water — perhaps not always commenting adequately on the plots of the stories I was writing about, nor quoting from them sufficiently. I hope in *Painted Desert, Green Shade* I have remedied this without going too far in the opposite direction. All the essays in this new book are assessments of individual authors, but I have attempted to link the work of the writer under discussion with that of others, to see his or her achievement as part of a continuing tradition, part of what many critics call the second golden age of children's literature. Writing on one particular author also focuses attention on themes of more general interest; thus Russell Hoban's work leads to a consideration of how the critic assesses picture books, Katherine Paterson's to comments on why and how literary awards are given, Jane Langton's and Lucy Boston's to thoughts on one use of fantasy — that which springs from a sense of a particular place, of history.

I continue to be fascinated by the differences and the similarities between the contemporary children's literature of American writers and their British counterparts. Why is it that British authors do not rival the Americans in the realistic depiction of everyday life? Why do Americans need to use the first person so often? How is it that some novelists, like Ursula Le Guin or Philippa Pearce, seem to transcend all national boundaries and write as if they stand apart from their native backgrounds, and speak with fluency to all? The subject is huge, and raises more questions than can be answered in any single collection of essays. The painted desert and the green shade of my title are exemplified by Virginia Hamilton and Lucy Boston — poles apart in their purposes, cast of mind, heritage, and interests, even if they meet in a concern for roots and are troubled by displacement from roots. In between lie an extraordinary diversity and richness of authors and books. In writing these essays I am trying to discover, among the award-winners and those who weren't even considered, just some of that diversity and richness — just a few of the painted deserts and the green shades of both Britain and America in contemporary fiction for the young.

References

MARGERY FISHER
Intent on Reading: A Critical Appraisal of Modern Fiction
Hodder 1961; revised edition 1964

BARBARA HARRISON
"Why Study Children's Literature?" *The Quarterly Journal of
the Library of Congress,* Fall 1981

PAUL HEINS
"Out on a Limb with the Critics" *The Horn Book Magazine,*
June 1970

C. S. LEWIS
An Experiment in Criticism Cambridge 1961

BERTHA MAHONY MILLER
Editorial, *The Horn Book Magazine* November 1939

DAVID REES
The Marble in the Water Horn Book 1980; Boydell & Brewer
1980

ROGER ROSENBLATT
"The Odd Pursuit of Teaching Books" *Time Magazine,* March
28, 1983

JOHN ROWE TOWNSEND
A Sense of Story Longman 1971; Lippincott 1971; revised edition, as *A Sounding of Storytellers* Kestrel 1979; Lippincott
1979

Green Thought in a Green Shade

L. M. BOSTON

It was like nowhere else, because while most houses are built to shut out everything but the inmates, to close doors and draw curtains equally against the cold winds from the edge of space and the curiosity of the neighbors, to make a cozy den where everything is yours and under your own control, Green Knowe was full of mysteries. Certainly it was welcoming and comfortable and rejoicing and gay, but one had the feeling that behind the exciting colors and shapes of its ancient self there might be surprises from the unknown universe; that the house was on good terms with that, too, and had no intention of shutting out the ununderstandable. Of course it was largely time. Surely the difference between Now and Not-now is the most teasing of all mysteries, and if you let in a nine-hundred-year dose of time, you let in almost everything.

Thus Lucy Boston, in *An Enemy at Green Knowe*, describes the setting of almost all her children's books — a country house so old that its chimneys date back to the Norman Conquest, and its gardens so lovingly cared for over the centuries that they seem timeless. It also happens to be where she actually lives, a manor-house near Cambridge: it is indeed one of the oldest inhabited houses in England. An author may well count herself fortunate to have such a rich background to draw upon.

Neil Philip, in an essay called "Fantasy: Double Cream or Instant Whip?" writes of the stillness at the center of Lucy

Boston's novels. This stillness comes from the presence of the house, steeped in history, on almost every page of the Green Knowe books, and the surrounding landscape, quiet, intensely English, as old as the fabric of the building itself. (A room in *An Enemy at Green Knowe* is described as being "fully occupied with its own quietness, as if that were something active," a remark which could apply equally well to the books themselves.) This stillness too is underlined by the character of the owner of the house, Mrs. Oldknow; it is a masterly stroke to present her as an elderly woman, so that she mirrors the qualities of where she lives— calm, experience, wisdom. To have made her sprightly and youthful would have produced a jarring and unpleasant contrast. A second factor which underlines the stillness is the character of the children around whom the stories revolve, particularly Mrs. Oldknow's great-grandson, Tolly, and the Chinese refugee boy, Ping. Tolly and Ping are reserved, polite, gentle people, a bit colorless in fact, often observers of the action rather than protagonists. There is a considerable quantity of drama and excitement in the narratives of some of the Green Knowe books, especially *A Stranger at Green Knowe* and *An Enemy at Green Knowe*, but the house, the children, and the old lady provide such a framework of tranquillity and good sense that Lucy Boston's writing often seems more like a meditation than an account of events; it is, to quote Marvell's poem, "The Garden," like "a green thought in a green shade."

John Rowe Townsend, in *Written for Children*, finds Lucy Boston weak in the portrayal of character and in the handling of narrative, and he suggests that her best work is not to be found in the Green Knowe novels, but in *The Sea Egg*. I agree with him. Characterization is not her strongest point — the children often seem more imagined than real, with their curiously adult insights and dialogue; they are "literary" creations. The structures of the first three Green Knowe books are loose, somewhat aimless; and *The Sea Egg* is undoubtedly her masterpiece. But John Rowe Townsend is perhaps too severe. *A Stranger at Green Knowe* and

An Enemy at Green Knowe are tightly structured, and Mrs. Oldknow is a particularly convincing creation. She is probably a self-portrait: it might be difficult for the author, having chosen to write so much about her own house and to make its owner a woman of roughly the same age as herself (she did not begin to write for children until she was in her sixties), to present Mrs. Oldknow as other than reflecting her own values, feelings, and thought processes. In *An Enemy at Green Knowe* Mrs. Oldknow says to Melanie Powers:

> I don't want comfortable pictures. I prefer them to have a nip of otherness, like life. In a house like this there is room for questions as well as answers.

"A nip of otherness, like life" is interesting; it expresses the essence of all her books, of the author herself. It was used by Sidney Robbins* as the title of an essay on Lucy Boston: he sees it as a key phrase that explains the author's intentions, why the house was not built "to shut out everything but the inmates, to close doors and draw curtains," but to have "room for questions as well as answers," and "that behind the exciting colors and shapes of its ancient self there might be surprises from the unknown universe." He says:

> It is this edge of fear and strangeness that makes the writer's vision so imaginatively compelling, so different from a time-locked, conservative clinging on to the past, but equally important in her vision are elements that are "welcoming and comfortable and rejoicing and gay."

It would be easy to make Green Knowe sound like a privileged bastion of outdated, reactionary attitudes, but Lucy Boston avoids this, as successfully as she avoids the lure of escapism, of using the house as a way of expressing nostalgia for a cozy, safe, long-dead rural past. If Green Knowe is

---

*Robbins had a superb knack for choosing exactly the right quotations in his essay on Lucy Boston. I have to admit that I have on occasion quoted the same passages.

a symbol at all, it is of life itself — a rich blend of experience and memory, questions and answers, "a nip of otherness" that is not always pleasant. In her particular use of an ancient country house, its gardens, and the English landscape, Lucy Boston shows that she belongs to the mainstream of great modern British writers of fantasy for children, with Mary Norton, Philippa Pearce, Alan Garner, Penelope Lively, and Penelope Farmer. *The Borrowers, Tom's Midnight Garden, The Owl Service, The House in Norham Gardens,* and *Year King* are all major works of fantasy that are exceptionally strong in their sense of place, of houses, of landscape; in *A Stranger at Green Knowe* and *An Enemy at Green Knowe* place has a similar importance, and a similar quality of high literary excellence.

High literary excellence: Lucy Boston's writing abilities are the equal of Paula Fox, of Philippa Pearce. Few books have an opening as superb as *The Sea Egg:*

> The sea was smooth and blue, like a looking glass reflecting the sky, and was slowly sinking back from the beach with hardly a ripple.
>
> It was a magical morning with a silence like all the secrets in the world and a light like happiness.

It isn't just the beauty of the language that strikes us here, but also its function — in two sentences the scene is set, the whole mood of the book suggested. And here is Ping, in *A Stranger at Green Knowe,* watching Hanno the gorilla in his cage at the London zoo:

> The cage was just big enough for him to take a bound from corner to corner, or he could stretch to his full height on the platform and touch the ceiling. It was as if Ping were shut up for life in a bathroom. The walls were tiled and the floor concrete. He had a horror of concrete. . . . He had lived on it in refugee camps that were often warehouses or railway sheds. . . . It was either deathly cold or mercilessly hot and had a hateful feeling under one's fingers, like rust.

As Sidney Robbins comments: "The link-up between their two experiences of displacement, of homelessness, is immediate and explicit; one refugee is here able to understand another refugee." The use of concrete as the immediate link is very effective, and striking, too, are the simile "like rust" and the phrase "shut up for life in a bathroom." I could continue with dozens of quotations, but one more will suffice. Few authors have the ability to evoke the senses as well as Lucy Boston; there are whole pages in *The Chimneys of Green Knowe* (published in America as *Treasure of Green Knowe*) and in *The River at Green Knowe* that appeal to one's sight, sound, touch, smell, or taste. Fear is often suggested in this way, as in this passage from *The River at Green Knowe:*

> They found themselves in what had once been a fine room. There were high windows on three sides, letting in a bottle-green light through the ivy blinds. The handsome plaster ceiling was still further decorated by small patches of twinkling watered silk where the river managed to play its flashing mirrors through gaps in the leaves. Opposite the balcony had been another pair of double doors, now missing, as were the fireplaces and all the doors in the house, so that on going through to the wide stair well and its banistered landings, one had the impression of a continuous but much alcoved room from ground floor to roof. Cobwebs hung everywhere as if the owners had left muslin curtains to molder away through the years. Dead leaves and straw littered the floors; shiny snail tracks climbed the walls. The children crept round apprehensively, greatly oppressed by that feeling in empty houses that if you think nobody lives there, *you are wrong*. Dust and silence, and boards that creaked, not when you trod on them, but minutes afterward behind you. Ida's heart began to feel tight. She was looking across the stairs into an open doorway, where a shadow was moving on the wall, when she felt a sharp rap on the back of her hand, as if someone had thrown a pebble.

> Something thudded on the floor. Ida clutched Oskar, and they bent down to look.
>
> "It's an owl pellet," said Oskar, laughing. "There must be an owl here and he spat at us."

In *The Children of Green Knowe* we meet Tolly, a lonely child — isolation and displacement are characteristics shared by most of the children in the Green Knowe stories — on his first visit to his great-grandmother:

> He wished he had a family like other people — brothers and sisters, even if his father were away. His mother was dead. He had a stepmother but he hardly knew her and was miserably shy of her.

Mrs. Oldknow is also an isolate; she and Tolly have at once a common bond. Tolly finds playthings in the house that belonged to three Oldknow children of the seventeenth century who died of bubonic plague; at a number of points in the book he meets them and makes friends with them. It's a time-slip tale, one in which people from the past are transferred to the present, rather than the other way round. The idea is repeated in other novels in the Green Knowe series, and in *The Stones of Green Knowe* the transfer works both ways; past comes alive in the present, and the present-day children visit the past. The quality of the writing in *The Children of Green Knowe* is excellent, but the narrative is fragmentary; it is really a collection of short, self-contained episodes, with the presence of Tolly, Mrs. Oldknow, and the house as the links. One is left with the feeling, at the end, that although Lucy Boston knew very well how to write, she didn't yet know how to write a novel.

The same unsatisfactory construction is also to be found in *Treasure of Green Knowe* and *The River at Green Knowe*, but in other ways both books show an improvement on the first. In *Treasure of Green Knowe* the time-slip to the past is the eighteenth century; there is more suspense and excitement, more of a real story than in *The Children of Green Knowe*. The villainy of the servant, Caxton, is particularly well-rendered, and so is the battle of wits between the blind girl, Susan, and her foolish, overprotective mother. When the house catches on fire, and Susan and the black servant, Jacob, make their way out by climbing down inside a chimney, the writing has a dramatic quality that was absent from the first book. Here, for once, Susan's blindness is an asset: "— she must feel for finger and foothold and balance, and unlike Jacob, she could shut her eyes against the smarting smoke and hot sparks without any disadvantage." What it is like to be blind has often been done well in contemporary children's fiction — *Goldengrove* by Jill Paton Walsh and *Annerton Pit* by Peter Dickinson are two other novels that present convincing creations of blind people.

In *The River at Green Knowe*, there is an entirely different set of characters. The house has been let for the summer to two strange middle-aged women who feel Green Knowe needs some young people; they send for Dr. Maud's great-niece, Ida, and apply to The Society for the Promotion of Summer Holidays for Displaced Children who promptly send them Oskar and Ping. The adventures in the past occur more in the surrounding landscape than in the house. It is the weakest book in the series in its narrative structure, but Lucy Boston shows a gift for comedy that does not frequently appear in her other novels:

> Dr. Maud was a shortsighted woman who never straightened her back, but moved about at the right height for consulting other books wherever she had laid them. When not reading, her attention was on the ground as if expecting that something very interesting there might catch her eye. She had spent much of her life digging up old cities and graves in deserts and shaly hillsides, and had got into the habit of searching the ground for fragments. She could not bear a vacuum cleaner because it left her nothing to look at.

Her equally odd friend, Sybilla Bun, has a passion for food and cooking —

> She was not unlike a hen in many ways, especially on the rare occasions when she ran, for instance, after the

bus. She chortled over her food and sometimes bowed gravely to it several times, looking at it first with one eye and then with the other before she ate. Her clothes were all fuss and flummery . . .

A Stranger at Green Knowe, which was awarded the Carnegie Medal in 1961, shows that Lucy Boston had at last conquered the narrative problem; it was a wise decision to abandon the idea of time-slip and replace it with a story set entirely in the twentieth century with a single, continuous action. The main character is a gorilla, Hanno — he is clearly based on Guy, the famous gorilla at the London Zoo, and the emotional impetus for the novel seems to come from the author's sense of disgust at seeing this beautiful and magnificent creature locked up in a cage. *A Stranger at Green Knowe* is one of those rare works of fiction that makes us think well beyond the confines of the story; if the reader has never before considered that keeping wild beasts in cages so that humans can gawp at them is immoral, this book will undoubtedly shake his complacency. Underneath the words throughout there is a tone of barely concealed anger; *A Stranger at Green Knowe*, in fact, is almost a polemic — but the author never forgets that her primary concern is artistic creation, the writing of a good story. Her feelings are always controlled, and used with immense skill to give an emotional edge, a disturbing sense of unease, to the words she uses. The plot is simple: Hanno escapes from the zoo and arrives at Green Knowe, where he lives for a short time in a dense thicket of bamboo. Only Ping knows he is there, and the two form a kind of relationship — Hanno seems to regard the Chinese boy as a baby gorilla, and Ping is content to play that role. One of the book's achievements is that Hanno never ceases to be a gorilla, awesome and terrifying; he is not given any sentimental human characteristics, so Ping, therefore, in his contact with the creature, is in a situation of great danger — one casual blow from the gorilla's arm could kill him. The police and the zoo people inevitably discover Hanno's whereabouts and he is shot dead. It is one of two possible endings; the more depressing alternative would be to have him sent back to his cage at the zoo. The question of whether death is preferable to life imprisonment is raised here; Hanno, Ping thinks, *opted* for the former —

"He's dead," he said clearly and too composedly. "It's all right. That is how much he didn't want to go back. I saw him choose."

The parallel between Ping's displacement and Hanno's is beautifully underlined at the end of the book when Mrs. Oldknow says to Ping —

"I wonder how much *you* mind 'going back,' as you said about Hanno. Would you like to live here with Tolly and me? Because I really feel I can't do without you."

— thus giving the story some kind of happy ending and a sense that at least one piece of justice has been done. It is not until the end that one realizes how apt is the curious way the book opens; the first twenty-five pages, which are an account of Hanno's first few years, free in the jungle before he is captured, do not at first sight seem relevant to the rest of the narrative, however important they are in making the contrast with his captivity as clear as possible. They are more than a realistic portrayal of the behavior of gorillas in the wild; they act as a metaphor for Ping's infant life (about which we hear very little) before he became a displaced person. Living at Green Knowe with Mrs. Oldknow restores to him the freedom he has lost. *A Stranger at Green Knowe* sets out to explore the idea that an animal and a human can equally "be stripped of everything that went with it, of which its instincts were an inseparable part, and that you could have just its little body in a space of nothingness" (these words are Ping's reactions to his visit to the zoo) and it presents a totally convincing case for saying that it is just as evil to do it to animals as it is to do it to humans.

In all the books the most stable, enduring element has been the house. Within its walls past and present are reconciled; the lonely old woman and the displaced child come

happily together; Hanno finds liberty, if only for a while. In
An Enemy at Green Knowe the house itself is threatened.
A Dr. Melanie Powers moves into the district; she is, apparently, interested in finding out whether any books of
Wolfgang Vogel, who lived at Green Knowe in the seventeenth century, are still in the house. Dr. Vogel was an expert on witchcraft and his attempts to practice black magic
led to his death. Miss Powers is a twentieth-century witch,
and it soon becomes evident that she is not so much interested in Dr. Vogel as in obtaining Green Knowe for herself.
She tries to break up the alliance between Mrs. Oldknow
and the children, then hypnotizes the old lady into thinking she doesn't want her own house any longer. When these
efforts fail, the attack becomes more direct. Miss Powers
conjures up a plague of maggots which destroys Mrs. Oldknow's beloved roses, but the maggots are eaten by birds;
the house is then menaced by scores of cats that kill the
birds and by snakes that swarm everywhere, including Mrs.
Oldknow's armchair, and, finally, during an eclipse of the
sun, an army of "fingers of some dreadful unknown sub-
stance" starts to tear off the roof-tiles and almost kills Mrs.
Oldknow with a dislodged stone. "If hatred could be seen at
work, it might look like that" the author comments. The
house is saved and Melanie Powers rendered harmless by
the efforts of the children and a witchcraft expert, Mr. Pope;
thus disproving Tolly's contention that Green Knowe
doesn't need guardians, that it can't have enemies: as Mrs.
Oldknow tells him, before Miss Powers appears on the
scene, "It has enemies, and it needs guarding all the
time" —

> "The very fact that it has lasted so long makes some
> people impatient. Time it went, they say, without fur-
> ther argument. The fact that it is different from any-
> where else, with memories and standards of its own,
> makes quite a lot of people very angry indeed. Things
> have no right to be different. Everything should be
> alike."

An Enemy at Green Knowe is the best novel of the six in my opinion. The narrative is very well handled, a superb demonstration of how to invoke excitement and suspense. Dr. Powers is a splendid creation — shallow, silly, and insidious, an illustration of the fact that evil can often be a product of selfish greed and small-mindedness. One suspects that the origin of the character may be in the author's feelings about unwelcome and insensitive members of the public who have visited the real house; Dr. Powers, as soon as she arrives, tries to poke her nose into several parts of Green Knowe that are obviously private —

> "I want to see every little corner." As she spoke, she pulled open a door. "Oh, a staircase. How interesting! And I hope you will show me the vaults."

Mrs. Oldknow, with some asperity — Lucy Boston's own annoyance, maybe — refuses. Green Knowe survives despite Miss Powers, though it was "the magnet of her cupidity;" its best guardian, Mrs. Oldknow, is, at the end of the story, alive and well, but the reader is aware that it is impossible for her to relax her vigilance. Penelope Lively, in "Children and Memory," says

> A house is a preservative, a record of the lives it has sheltered. No one has used place more effectively than Lucy Boston: the house and the garden in the Green Knowe books are her medium for talking about continuity.

But, just as the reader is led in *A Stranger at Green Knowe* to go outside the story and think about the morality of zoos, he is here also made to consider the book's implications: to realize that continuity cannot be taken for granted, that our heritage is always in danger of destruction.

The last of the series, *The Stones of Green Knowe,* was published some twelve years after the others and it is disappointing, though one might consider it a remarkable achievement for an author aged eighty-four. The plot is episodic, like the first three books, and some of the magic has disappeared from the writing. Chunks of information are not comfortably integrated into the text, and memorable insights and images are few. Its most interesting part shows the building of the house in Norman times, the first occasion stone was used at Green Knowe, and there are some nice humorous touches. Mrs. Oldknow, despite her age, is obviously aware of youthful fashion fads: she sees the Norman boy, Roger d'Aulneaux: he's dressed in the costume of his own period, but she mistakes him for Tolly. "Where did you get those clothes?" she asks. "I know there's been a jumble sale, but those are London's best." Indeed, they probably were!

Yet another terrible threat to Green Knowe — the effect of twentieth-century trash and pollution — is illustrated very well by using Roger's sense of what is missing from his world in today's world:

> There were no horses, no donkeys, no rabbits nor hares. No partridges rose up under his feet, no foxes were prowling, no wagtails running about, no ducks on the river, no herons, no swarms of goldfinches over the thistles, no heavy bumble-bees, and no butterflies. Consequently there was an unnaturally still dead air — he heard no rabbit-thudding, no small wings purring or large wings flapping, no quacking and splashing, no harsh cry from the heron, no tinkling sound, like Linnet's bracelets, from the goldfinches, no bumbling, no soft beat of butterflies' wings past his ear. There was only an occasional rook talking to itself in a melancholy way as it went over, and there were two swans on the river and a moorhen, and in the fields a few starlings. The world seemed nearly dead.

The Castle of Yew is a story for younger readers; the setting is presumably Green Knowe, but the house is not named. It is owned by an old lady, and the garden, in which most of the action takes place, is extensive and well cared for as in the Green Knowe books; there is also "a nip of otherness," a hint of the mysterious, even of menace:

> Empty gardens often seem to threaten an intruder, more so even than the wildest country, because they

are made to be private. And who can tell whether, for instance, a tunnel cut through a dense evergreen hedge will let you through, or close in and catch you in the middle?

When the children, Joseph and Robin, enter the garden, they discover they are only a few inches high — one is reminded a little of Mary Norton's *Borrowers* stories. Much of the narrative derives from the difficulties of being very small, particularly with the animals the boys encounter. There is a memorable confrontation with a cat: in this book, as in *An Enemy at Green Knowe*, cats are not seen as gentle domestic pets, but as cruel, selfish creatures; this cat has "curved hayfork claws" and its eyes are yellow with "a vertical black slit that was like a gap between curtains, and they stared terribly, without any expression." Though the prose in *The Castle of Yew* is much simpler than in the Green Knowe novels, with less complex sentences and unambiguous concepts, it is very good; Lucy Boston's abilities are in no way hampered by writing for the young child.

Nothing Said, The Fossil Snake, and *The Guardians of the House* are short pieces of less importance than *The Castle of Yew*, but *The Sea Egg*, also brief, is a remarkable tour de force. It is the story of Toby and Joe, on holiday by the sea in Cornwall; they buy from a lobsterman a stone that is egg-shaped, knowing that it is no ordinary stone because none can be exactly the shape of an egg: it *is* an egg, in fact, and it hatches. Out of it comes a strange sea-creature, Triton, who takes the boys on a series of fantastic underwater adventures. The book is one long prose-poem from beginning to end and is a delight to read; in modern children's fiction only Paula Fox in *The Slave Dancer* describes the sea and changes of weather as well as Lucy Boston does here:

> Then all was quiet, except for that murmurous half telling, half withholding of tremendous secrets that the sea would keep up all night.

Onomatopoeia, assonance, subtle rhythm, in this passage are exceptionally satisfying:

13

> From distant caves came a steady boom, boom, as of quarrying. Now and again a particularly powerful wave would form itself with a long foaming head and muscle its way through the tumult with a tearing roar, throwing up stones ahead of it. The air re-echoed with toppling crashes, whip cracks, and the high rattle of shingle over a continuous fiendish rumble.

The sea is present on almost every page, yet the lack of repetitiveness is astonishing; the fascination of its unpredictable, constant changes is suggested in one telling phrase after another in words as unpredictable and constantly changing in pattern as the ocean itself. The sea can be "cold and fish-coloured," a wave can be "a swirl of sea lace" or, on another occasion, "like someone leaving in a petty temper." Seaweed after rain is "plump and smelling of iodine;" in moonlight "rocks jutting out of sea and sand were like watchers or crouching animals," and the rise and fall, the use of internal rhyme, is perfection here —

> . . . . there was the sea, huge and wide and blue, and so full of light that it seemed hardly to be there at all, but it heaved gently, as if it breathed in its sleep, and whispered in an echoey way, both near and very far off.

The ability to render in words the sheer physical pleasure of the senses is one of the great strengths of *The Sea Egg* — coolness, heat, the sensation of water on the skin when swimming, landscape that fills the eye, the great variety of sounds the sea produces, the smell of what is left on the beach when the tide recedes. It matters little that the plot lacks some of the dramatic momentum of *A Stranger at Green Knowe* and *An Enemy at Green Knowe*, that its characterization, though competent, is not outstanding; the power of a particular place holds the reader totally.

The power of a particular place: this is what distinguishes Lucy Boston from other writers, gives her stories their singular richness, produces the quality of stillness at their centers. One should say, finally, that the illustrations by her son, Peter Boston, are striking visual interpretations of many of the big moments: the appearance of Hanno at the French doors of Green Knowe, making Mrs. Oldknow and Ping look like dwarfs; Roger staring at Green Knowe as it is now; the two boys undressing on the moonlit beach in *The Sea Egg*. He conveys, at his best, not just the essence of the words, but what is going on beneath and around them — the green shade of the green thought.

References

L. M. BOSTON
The Children of Green Knowe Faber 1954; Harcourt 1955
The Chimneys of Green Knowe Faber 1958; in America, as *Treasure of Green Knowe*, Harcourt 1958
The River at Green Knowe Faber 1959; Harcourt 1959
A Stranger at Green Knowe Faber 1961; Harcourt 1961
An Enemy at Green Knowe Faber 1964; Harcourt 1964
The Castle of Yew Bodley Head 1965; Harcourt 1965
The Sea Egg Faber 1967; Harcourt 1967
Nothing Said Faber 1971; Harcourt 1971
The Guardians of the House Bodley Head 1974; Atheneum 1975
The Fossil Snake Bodley Head 1975; Atheneum 1976
The Stones of Green Knowe Bodley Head 1976; Atheneum 1976

PETER DICKINSON
Annerton Pit Gollancz 1977; Atlantic/Little, Brown 1977

PENELOPE FARMER
Year King Chatto 1977; Atheneum 1977

PAULA FOX
The Slave Dancer Bradbury 1973; Macmillan, London, 1974

ALAN GARNER
The Owl Service Collins, London, 1967; Walck 1968

PENELOPE LIVELY
"Children and Memory" in *The Horn Book Magazine*, August 1973
The House in Norham Gardens Heinemann 1974; Dutton 1974

ANDREW MARVELL
"The Garden" first published in 1681

MARY NORTON
   The Borrowers Dent 1952; Harcourt 1953
JILL PATON WALSH
   Goldengrove Macmillan, London, 1972; Farrar 1972
PHILIPPA PEARCE
   Tom's Midnight Garden Oxford 1958; Lippincott 1959
NEIL PHILIP
   "Fantasy: Double Cream or Instant Whip?" in *Signal* 35, May
   1981
SIDNEY ROBBINS
   "A Nip of Otherness, Like Life" in *Children's literature in ed-
   ucation,* November 1971
JOHN ROWE TOWNSEND
   Written for Children Garnett Miller 1965; Lothrop 1967; re-
   vised edition Penguin 1974; Lippincott 1974

Discreet Charm of the Bourgeoisie

M. E. KERR

M. E. Kerr is a subtle and talented writer with a great number of interesting, wise things to say, though a superficial glance would suggest that her work is unremarkable. There is little description of place or sensitivity to the changes of weather: the seaside setting, for instance, of *Love Is a Missing Person*, *Gentlehands*, and *I'll Love You When You're More Like Me*, and the boarding school of *Is That You, Miss Blue?* show an environment in which wealthy upper middle-class people live in uneasy proximity to those much less well off, but the places themselves are never properly realized. What does this stretch of coast, or this school, look like? We are never told. The background of *Dinky Hocker Shoots Smack!* is New York City, Brooklyn Heights to be exact, but there is no particular flavor of that place in the book. Every one of her novels, with the exception of *Dinky Hocker Shoots Smack!* is a first person narration, and the "voice" is not well individualized: all the narrators, boy or girl, sound alike. This is a fault in Judy Blume's stories, and indeed in many American novels for children and young adults published in the past thirty years (since J. D. Salinger's *The Catcher in the Rye*, in fact). Here is Alan, the central character of *If I Love You, Am I Trapped Forever?*:

> While you're reading the next few paragraphs, it may help you to remember that I'm going to get what's coming to me. Just imagine that even as I write this first chapter about myself, unforeseen clouds are gathering in the distance.

17

> But at the beginning of this novel, I am Alan Bennett, age sixteen, and I have to come right out and tell you: I'm *the* most popular boy at Cayuta High. Very handsome. Very cool. Dynamite.

Suzy, the narrator of *Love Is a Missing Person,* talks in much the same manner, even if she is here saying something rather different:

> Your snazzier Slades don't even use words like "snazzy" — my mother calls them "tackyisms." I catch words and phrases like other people catch germs, and most of mine originate with Miss Gwendolyn Spring. She is a forty-eight-year-old, self-described nervous wreck, and my favorite friend and ally at the Seaville Free Library.

> I am Suzy, the Slade daughter the father chose *not* to take to New York to live with him. My mother actually gave him his choice of girls.

Four of the novels, *Little Little, I'll Love You When You're More Like Me, The Son of Someone Famous,* and *What I Really Think of You* use *two* first person narrators, each taking alternate chapters. This is a very artificial convention; not even original — Paul Zindel used it in *The Pigman* to better effect, as the voices of John and Lorraine at least sound different from each other. Alan's grandfather in the first paragraph of *If I Love You, Am I Trapped Forever?* says that "writing in the first person is like painting with watercolors: only small children and geniuses can do it well." He goes on to add that a first person story is "a self-involved word-salad." Self-involved word-salads would not be a fair description of M. E. Kerr's prose style, but her continual use of the first person certainly shows up the limitations of the device.

Repetitiveness is another fault — why, for instance, are there four different men in four different novels all surnamed Baird? And so is the reliance on melodrama. Few of the adults come over as attractive people; the parents of the main characters are nearly always selfish, prudish, conventional, overprotective, unimaginative, rarely allowing their offspring any privacy, and many of them drink too much. Little Little's mother has all of these faults, and so has Mrs. Blossom in *The Son of Someone Famous*; Mrs. Hocker, though not conventional nor addicted to alcohol, is a selfish prude and quite revolting in the way she interferes with the young people's private lives. Mrs. Slade is certainly not overprotective, but she suffers from all the other defects; Mrs. Boyle in *Gentlehands*, who is more sympathetic than most of the others, rarely drinks, is genuinely fond of her son, and is willing to give him space, but she, too, is conventional, unimaginative, and prudish. Melodrama abounds: the destruction of Little Little's birthday cake, the cat leaping out of the coffin at a funeral in *I'll Love You When You're More Like Me*, the kidnapping of Guy Pegler in *What I Really Think of You*, Adam's mother's attempted elopement and death in *The Son of Someone Famous*, Alan's father's drunken behavior in a smart restaurant in *If I Love You, Am I Trapped Forever?* It is true that the plots rarely hinge on melodramatic occurrences, but in many of the stories too much happens at once at the climax, and the final, sometimes unnecessary, event is often melodramatic.

All M. E. Kerr's books, however, are better than they appear to be at first sight. The narrative is frequently exciting and tightly knit, the dialogue excellent; the sardonic and caustic sense of humor is original, telling; there is wisdom and sharp observation of reality in one statement after another:

> "If you love someone," my mother said, "you have to let them know it. Don't play hard to get. Love is a verb." (*If I Love You, Am I Trapped Forever?*)

Which makes a neat contrast with Wally Witherspoon's realization that parental disapproval is a way of saying "I'll love you when you're more like me." In *Love Is a Missing Person* there is

> "Wouldn't it make you mad, though, if you were a black girl, seeing white girls go after your men?"
> Miss Spring said quickly and flatly, "Yes."

and this brief comment on Mrs. Hocker in *Dinky Hocker Shoots Smack!* is accurate and devastating:

> The community was a little like Mrs. Hocker: she meant well and everything, but she always seemed to be there *after* the damage was done.

In *Is That You, Miss Blue?* we have:

> "A woman would never be God," Cardmaker said. "Not any God of *this* universe. Her maternal instincts would prevent it."

and this exchange in *Little Little* is delightful:

> I remembered a day under our raft last August when Jarvis Allen told me he'd be willing to make out with me, so I'd have the experience. I told him thanks, anyway, but I wanted my first experience to lead to my second, not to discourage me from ever doing it again
> . . .

Sometimes the insight is less briefly put, but is nevertheless as forceful. Here is Brenda Belle Blossom, in *The Son of Someone Famous*, realizing that the conventional ideas of sexual attraction she has heard about are quite different from the real thing:

> I do know that I rode along beside him thinking: "He is *beautiful!*" and everything I'd learned about male/female relationships at my mother's knee told me there was something wrong about that. The male is supposed to be thinking that; the female is supposed to be thinking: I'm glad I am so beautiful that he wants to be with me.

Alan, too, in *If I Love You, Am I Trapped Forever?* grows up a little when his mother says that his father was the only man she ever loved; he realizes, for the first time, that his parents were once his age and experienced the same emotions — always a difficult idea for a child or an adolescent to accept, and rarely so well put as it is here:

> It came as a shock. I never thought of my mother loving him that much. Whenever I thought about my

father at all, I thought about him walking out on us, and leaving my mother to face the town . . . and the prospect of bringing me up without a father.

"Love" isn't a word that conjures up a vision of one's own parents. If you think of love at all, in connection with their feelings about each other, you think of it as something that might have had something to do with them a long time ago. But you don't think of it as the same kind of love *you're* experiencing; they're too old, and in their day it was kid stuff, being in love. It wasn't deep, like it is now.

There are times, however, when the prose falters, when a clichéd simile replaces the cogent analysis, and such moments seem particularly poor when they are surrounded, as they often are, by so much good writing:

I didn't say anything. I could feel things begin to crumble inside, as though instead of internal organs there was a house of cards under my skin, and the top card had slipped. (*I'll Love You When You're More Like Me*)

With the exception of *Is That You, Miss Blue?* the concerns of the novels from *Dinky Hocker Shoots Smack!* to *I'll Love You When You're More Like Me* are all much the same, though each one involves a different kind of "problem": it would be wearisome to go over their plots, built up, as they are, mosaic-fashion, from the interests and worries of most teenagers — dating, clothes, clashes with parents, driving cars, the routines of school, friendships, falling in and out of love; but from *Gentlehands* onwards the narratives rely on less conventional elements, indeed the bizarre and outrageous come to dominate. Alan's difficulties in *If I Love You, Am I Trapped Forever?* are coming to terms with his absentee, divorced father and the fact that his girlfriend leaves him for a boy he regards as an ineffectual loser. In *The Son of Someone Famous*, Adam lives with his kindly but alcoholic granddad because he can't cope with his celebrated father, a well-known politician (who has an interesting similarity to Henry Kissinger); his girlfriend also has problems living with her widowed mother and widowed aunt. In *Love Is a Missing Person* Suzy's dilemmas are with her sister who is a drop-out, a thief, and ultimately a missing person — she disappears, probably with her black boy friend, and is never seen again. *I'll Love You When You're More Like Me* is the story of Wally Witherspoon's frustrating holiday romance with neurotic Sabra St. Amour, a teenage TV personality, and his attempts — successful in the end — to avoid a career in his father's business, that of an undertaker. Wally's friend, Charlie, is an interesting creation: he's gay, and, deciding to come out of the closet, unwisely tells everyone of his sexual orientation. It is a pity that the author, after beginning to explore this idea, doesn't seem to know how to integrate the character properly into the plot; but her concern for persecuted minority groups, for people who are gentle and sympathetic but who do not fit into approved behavior patterns — the radical sympathizer that P. John Knight turns into in *Dinky Hocker Shoots Smack!* for example, or The American Diminutives in *Little Little* — is nowhere better illustrated than with Charlie; "honesty," Wally comments, "has its own rewards: ostracism and disgrace." Charlie's mother wants the priest to exorcise him; his father hits him and breaks his nose. Wally's father refers to Charlie as "limp wrist; weak sister; flying saucer; fruitstand; thweetheart; fairy tale; cupcake, on and on," and Charlie says of himself:

> You can make straight A's and A+'s for ten years of school, and on one afternoon, in a weak moment, confess you think you're gay. What do you think you'll be remembered as thereafter? Not the straight-A student.

These comments are also right on the mark —

> Charlie says ever since the movies and television have been showing great, big, tough gays, to get away from the stereotype effeminates, he's been worse off than ever before. "Now I'm supposed to live up to some kind of big butch standard, where I can Indian-wrestle

anyone in the bar to the floor, or produce sons, or lift five-hundred pound weights over my head without my legs breaking."

"The media is trying to make it easier for your kind," I argued back.

"They're trying to make it easier for those of my kind who most resemble them," Charlie said.

The most successful of these books is the first, *Dinky Hocker Shoots Smack!* despite its plot being less well organized, more episodic than its successors. Tucker Woolf is the most appealing character in all M. E. Kerr's novels, a totally credible, ordinary fifteen-year-old boy, worried that his armpits smell, that he's unhappy on a date, that he has no small talk let alone scintillating conversation, depressed because he has no meaningful relationships. "My parents tell me what to do and I do it," he says. "And I tell my friends what I've done and they tell me what they've done. Are those relationships?" He thinks he'll become a librarian:

> "When I get nervous, I go to the library and hang around. The libraries are filled with people who are nervous. You can blend in with them there. You're bound to see someone more nervous than you are in a library. Sometimes the librarians themselves are more nervous than you are. I'll probably be a librarian for that reason. Then if I'm nervous on the job, it won't show. I'll just stamp books and look up things for people and run back and forth to the staff room sneaking smokes until I get hold of myself. A library is a great place to hide."

The story begins with Tucker advertising for someone to adopt his cat; his father has developed an allergy to cats. This leads to his friendship with Dinky Hocker, an obese, unloved and rejected girl — her mother is much more preoccupied with rehabilitating junkies than with loving her daughter; she's a character remarkably like Mrs. Jellyby in Dickens's *Bleak House*, so involved with converting the natives of Borrioboola-Gha to Christianity that she totally neglected her own children. This friendship introduces Tucker to Dinky's cousin, Natalia, with whom he very slowly begins to form a relationship, despite Mrs. Hocker's interference and disapproval and his own parents' lack of comprehension. "Are you falling for Natalia?" his mother asks him. He doesn't know; his reply is a shout of exasperation: "Do we have to settle it right now, over hamburgers?" Tucker's feelings are summed up in the words of an old Beatles' song he is fond of — "You ask me if my love will grow. I don't know. I don't know." His mother puts him in a no-win situation with these comments:

> "You shouldn't monopolize her time if you're not serious about her."
> "I am serious about her."
> "Have you told her that?"
> "I guess she knows."
> "I hope you're not too serious about her."

But it ends happily: the relationship does grow, and the adults give it their blessing. The author remembers, as so many writers of young adult novels do not remember or refuse to admit, that a fifteen-year-old boy is a sexual person: "His body would actually feel her presence and remember the way she could affect him when they kissed or danced together;" but his emotions are not "the kind of sensation he had sometimes after reading sexy parts in novels, or while seeing sexy photographs, nor was it like feelings he had after sexy daydreams. It was just this strong feeling, completely physical, done with eyes." (In *If I Love You, Am I Trapped Forever?* the relationship between Alan and Leah is sexual, though Alan says he doesn't want to describe in detail "the very personal things that take place . . . I'm not writing this book for a bunch of voyeurs.") The romance between Tucker and Natalia is one of the most convincing portrayals of adolescent love in contemporary young adult fiction, as fine as the teenage relationships in Jill Chaney's novels — *Half a Candle, Mottram Park, The Buttercup*

Field. Dinky Hocker Shoots Smack! is, for a first novel, a remarkable achievement.

Is That You, Miss Blue? stands apart from the other stories in that almost all the drama revolves around the adults; the teenage protagonist and her friends are observers of the main action. The problems and emotional crises in, for example, *If I Love You, Am I Trapped Forever?*, *The Son of Someone Famous*, and *Love Is a Missing Person* are partly those of the adult characters (it is rare to find this in a novel for young people) but in *Is That You, Miss Blue?* they dominate events. The setting, too, is different; this time we are inside a snobbish private school for girls that places a strong emphasis on religious education. There is the usual gallery of misfits and eccentrics one has come to expect from M. E. Kerr — a dragon of a headmistress; Miss Balfour who does nothing but look in a mirror all day long; Agnes Thatcher who is deaf and dumb; Carolyn Cardmaker, as sharp-tongued and unhappy as Dinky Hocker — but the real oddity is the science mistress, Miss Blue. Miss Blue is a faded, pathetic spinster given to reading the Book of Revelations aloud and sitting for hours in front of a portrait of Mary, Queen of Scots. She thinks Christ comes into her room and talks to her. She is — it's a little hard to believe — the best teacher in the school. The narrator, Flanders Brown, at first thinks of her as merely somebody to poke fun at, but she comes to like her and feel sorry for her. "Without even knowing her, I sensed she needed protection," Flanders says, perhaps because she has some intuitive awareness of Miss Blue's vicarious enjoyment of suffering and martyrdom:

> There was the usual flush to her face, but the chin was thrust forward in a combative attitude, and there was a certain borrowed agony in her eyes, as though she was undertaking some of what she imagined to be Agnes' burden simply by walking alongside her.

Miss Blue *is* martyred. The climax of the story — ironic, in that this is a church school — is her dismissal by the head-mistress for her supposed religious mania. Cardmaker neatly sums up the writer's message:

> "Anyone who flaunts her religion all over the place has to take the chance someone else might not be tickled to death with the idea, but she should still have the right to flaunt it."

Is That You, Miss Blue? does not echo characters found in other novels, nor does it suffer from melodrama. The irony and the perceptiveness of its observations are first-rate; there is also a total grip on the narrative structure and some splendid writing:

> She looks like an old mud turtle which someone has stood upright and put a dress on. She wrote a sentence across a blackboard that she said she wanted us all to memorize. It was: SIMPLICITY IS THE KEYNOTE OF REFINEMENT. She broke her piece of chalk with the strength it took to write it.

It is a very good book.

The publication of *Gentlehands* showed a new direction in M. E. Kerr's work, and a reaction from the critics some-what different from the usual chorus of praise. At first sight, this story appears to have ingredients similar to those of the previous novels, the customary portrayal of adoles-cent gaucheness and intensity of feeling: teenage working-class Buddy Boyle in love with an unsuitable rich girl, and at loggerheads with his parents. The new material is the presence and function in the plot of Buddy's grandfather, a German who emigrated after the Second World War. Herr Trenker lives alone; he's a nice man, educated, cultured, with a fondness for animals and a considerable understand-ing of young people. Buddy moves in with him, and Grand-father begins to provide all the emotional and material aspects of life the boy does not have in his own home. At a party at his girlfriend's house, Buddy meets Nick De Lucca, an investigative journalist whose personality and ap-pearance are repellent, a little reminiscent of Uriah Heep.

De Lucca is a Jew whose sister was tortured and killed by the Nazis; his mission in life is to track down and expose her murderer who is responsible for the deaths of thousands of other Jews. In a newspaper article, he names Buddy's grandfather as the wanted man. Without waiting for Herr Trenker to defend himself, the townspeople side with De Lucca; anti-German hatred erupts, and Trenker's dog has its throat slit. Buddy reacts in disbelief and anger, but it turns out that his grandfather *is* the Nazi killer . . .

The story suddenly ends at this point, leaving the reader confused, indeed outraged. This is *not* one of those novels Ted Hughes would call a hospital where we heal. What was the author's intention in writing a scenario such as this? To make us realize that Nazi war criminals loved their families and their pets? We know this; the facts can be found in any book on the subject. To make us feel compassion for such men? Herr Trenker is a man *no one* could pity. De Lucca and the townspeople come over very negatively; does the author wish to suggest that racist hatred exists in all human beings, not just in easily identifiable enemies who are now part of history? Racism may exist, is perhaps buried, in the most liberal of any of us, but few nations have such a bad record as Germany in the 1930s and 1940s; not many people have *acted* on their racist feelings as the Nazis did. Is it M. E. Kerr's intention to say "it could happen anywhere"?

Easily the worst aspect of the story is its abrupt ending, which makes it impossible to assess what the author is trying to say, and leaves no room for any depiction of how Buddy comes to terms with what has happened; he — and therefore the reader — is left in moral and psychological confusion. A novel for children or teenagers ought to differ from a novel for adults in this: if the conclusion is without hope, the adolescent protagonist should, as in Robert Cormier's novels, be able to understand why that is so and be prepared for it. The young have to learn about death, the fact that the world is often messy and corrupt, that there are no certitudes; but their literature should help to strengthen them so that they can cope with disaster. The final sentence of *Gentlehands* shows the author running away — "I just wanted to leave everything about that summer behind me." There is strong characterization in *Gentlehands*, humor, well-paced narrative, the perceptions one has come to expect from M. E. Kerr, but the reader feels just as Buddy Boyle does: he wants to leave everything about this novel behind him. A story that produces such a reaction is a battlefield where we get injured.

Little Little is not totally satisfactory, though the reasons for this are different from the failings of *Gentlehands*. The subject matter this time is dwarfs, and once again the author wishes to make the reader aware of the difficulties members of a minority group have in living effectively when confronted with the way the world behaves and operates. Life isn't designed to accommodate the problems of midgets:

> When I wake up in my room in Wilton, the first thing I see is myself reflected in the full-length mirror across the room. I am in my little bed, made especially for me by a Wilton carpenter, and next to it is the bureau he built to my size, and the desk and chair. I know the real world begins just outside my door and down the hall, where the bathroom confronts me with the toilet and the sink, which take great effort to reach, and I am again like a mushroom growing in a forest inhabited by giants.

Little Little La Belle and Sydney Cinnamon, both dwarfs, have to put up with ostracism and indifference, and there is also the question of whether to resist or succumb to exploitation by the owners of freak shows, demands for appearances on TV commercials, being used as mascots by sports teams; they are also bothered by problems adolescents of the usual size are confronted with — in Little Little's case, overprotective and snobbish parents, who disapprove of her friendship with Sydney because he has sold himself to showbiz interests. He takes part in commercials for a firm of pest exterminators, and is the mascot of the Wilton Bombers; he performs at half-time in the games as a cockroach —

"They're filthy things!" Laura Gwen said.

"They aren't. People are," I said. "Roaches drag people's dirt around, not their own."

Mrs. La Belle hopes to marry Little Little off to a dwarf preacher called Little Lion — he's much more "respectable" than Sydney — but Little Little quite rightly refuses; Little Lion is a phoney.

It is the narrative, this time, that is the weakness. The story starts too slowly — the first fifty pages are mostly background information and rather aimless thinking aloud — and when it does begin to move, it is not much different from any of the other plots about the conflict between teenagers and their parents over boy friends and girl friends. M. E. Kerr's research shows through too obviously at times; there are constant references to books by other people about dwarfs. Although the story ends happily, with the La Belle parents defeated, and Little Little and Sydney enjoying their relationship, there is a depressed low-key feeling about the whole novel. Perhaps that is because there is nothing quite so incisive as, for example, the way the author sums up the homophobic reactions to Charlie in *I'll Love You When You're More Like Me,* and because she does not succeed in making Sydney and Little Little sympathetic enough as *people;* Sydney, in particular, comes over as hard, eager to play the exploiters' games, not very likeable. The cockroach shell is an effective symbol, but I wonder if the author really wanted him to have the characteristics of a cockroach: if she did, she's asking once again for too much from the reader.

The main characters in *What I Really Think of You* are once again misfits, this time the children of revivalist preachers. The structure of M. E. Kerr's books is almost becoming a formula: first-person narration by two people, class differences, corrupt and/or ineffective adults, some kind of oddity in the background of the central character that makes him or her an outcast. What next? Circus freaks, Hispanic fruitpickers, communists? Which is not to say that *What I Really Think of You* is a poor novel. The narrative moves along well; characterization is good, dialogue sparkling; and there is the usual crop of epigrammatic, witty comments about human behavior. "A parked car off somewheres in the woods carries three passengers," Arnelle Ringer says, "a boy, a girl, and Satan"; the problems of being a preacher's child are sadly summed up by Jesse Pegler —

> I was wondering why we couldn't just roll up our jeans around our ankles and run down to the beach, along the surf, hand in hand, and talk about something simple like who did what at school. . . .

— and this sentence is a masterly example of deliberate anti-climax:

> A time to be born, and a time to die, as the Bible tells it; a time to plant, and a time to pluck up that which is planted; a time to kill, and a time to heal; a time to break down . . . which is what happened to Bobby John's car that night, with Guy Pegler in it.

The author's attitude to born-again Christianity is skeptical though not totally antagonistic, but there is a great deal of contempt expressed through several characters for those in the revivalist movement who use their manipulative abilities to feather their own nests. The contrasts between the two preachers — Royal Ringer, minister of The Helping Hand Tabernacle, a crusty, brash, awkward man with no money, and Guy Pegler of the electric church, A Challenge Enterprise, smooth-talking and corrupted by money — are striking. Ringer's children find him difficult to live with but they remain loyal to him on the whole. Dr. Pegler's elder son abandons him, yet when the boy returns to the fold, he begins to lose his younger son, Jesse. Royal's daughter, Opal, wishes for a normal life, a boy friend, dates, status, but she is able to see that the "haves" aren't always enviable; the teenage couples she watches are "just like into the ark, in twos." Opal remains, to the end, an outsider, but she's capable ultimately of overcoming her envy and saying to mankind in general that "what she really thinks of you" is "I love you, yes I love you."

M. E. Kerr is one of the most gifted writers of novels for young adults to have emerged in the past decade. She is popular, too. Teenagers like her brisk style, her wit, the fast pace of the narratives — American teenagers, that is: their British counterparts, alas, have had little opportunity to enjoy her work as only two of her books are published in the United Kingdom, a sad state of affairs one hopes will soon be remedied. Her intelligence and her abilities are considerable, but there is a narrowness of range and a danger that she may be repeating herself. It is a little worrying that, of the nine novels she has published, only one — *Is That You, Miss Blue?* — is superior to her first, *Dinky Hocker Shoots Smack!* However, she is one of the few authors whose books for the young show adults as major, influential characters; this is a complete change from those novels of two or three decades ago in which parents and grandparents are dispensed with in the first chapter. The tensions in her stories frequently come from parent-child relationships — Dinky and Mrs. Hocker, Alan Bennett and his suddenly acquired father, Little Little and Mrs. La Belle, Sabra St. Amour and her mother. Also some of her most interesting scenes and insights occur when the teenager is drawn into the conflicts of adults who are not parents — Flan Brown and Miss Blue, Suzy Slade and Miss Spring, Adam and Billie Kay, the fading movie star. With the exception of *Love Is a Missing Person*, the relationships between the young people and their contemporaries can seem a quiet oasis, a needed escape from parental tensions and the problems of an adult milieu. The teenagers are often put through an experience in which they stop seeing adults as stereotypes of the older generation, and come to view them as complex individuals, capable of being hurt, selfish, manipulative, or sympathetic and loving. Her unique achievement is to place the adult right at the center of the teenage novel.

References

M. E. KERR

    Dinky Hocker Shoots Smack! Harper 1972; Gollancz 1973
    If I Love You, Am I Trapped Forever? Harper 1973
    The Son of Someone Famous Harper 1974; Gollancz 1975
    Is That You, Miss Blue? Harper 1975
    Love Is a Missing Person Harper 1975
    I'll Love You When You're More Like Me Harper 1977
    Gentlehands Harper 1978
    Little Little Harper 1982
    What I Really Think of You Harper 1982

JILL CHANEY

    Half a Candle Dobson 1968; Crown 1969
    Mottram Park Dobson 1970
    The Buttercup Field Dobson 1977

CHARLES DICKENS

    Bleak House first published in 1853

J. D. SALINGER

    The Catcher in the Rye Little, Brown 1951; Hamish Hamilton 1951

PAUL ZINDEL

    The Pigman Harper 1968; Bodley Head 1969

Little Bit of Ivory

BETSY BYARS

Betsy Byars is a prolific writer; almost every year since the late sixties she has produced a novel for children. With such a large output, one might expect to find a body of work with a considerable diversity in quality, a wide assortment of interests, differing structures, implied readers of varying ages. The surprise is that this is not so. Betsy Byars's novels are all much the same length (shorter, in fact, than many children's books), have similar structures, differ little in quality, and the implied reader is usually a child of between nine and twelve years old. Nor does the material of her books show much variety. She usually writes about children who are loners, or who have acute difficulties in their families or with their peer groups, who are forced to operate in trying situations that make them grow up a little. The narrowness of range is quite remarkable. Such comments could also apply to Judy Blume, but Betsy Byars's work shows what children who only read Judy Blume are in danger of missing — originality and inventiveness, lack of repetition, wit and good sense, a succinct prose style with terse, vivid perceptions and ironical observations of life. If any children's writer can be said, as Jane Austen commented about the themes and people in her own novels, to work on a "little bit (two inches wide) of ivory," it is Betsy Byars.

As in the novels of M. E. Kerr, adults are major figures in those of Betsy Byars, but they are not, as in *Is That You, Miss Blue?*, at the center of the action, the characters around whom the narrative revolves. They certainly influence events and people, but Betsy Byars's stories are the stories of the child protagonist. That child either has only one parent, as in *The Night Swimmers, The TV Kid, The Cybil War, The Cartoonist,* and *Good-bye, Chicken Little,* or has been abandoned temporarily by both parents — *The Midnight Fox, The House of Wings, Trouble River* — or is without parents at all — *The Pinballs* and *After the Goat Man.* Grandparents, therefore, assume an importance that is unusual in children's books, and often it is the grandparent who is one of the most memorable characters in the story, because he or she is strong, cross-grained, highly individual — *Trouble River, After the Goat Man, The House of Wings* — or weak, selfish and ineffectual — *The Cartoonist, The Cybil War,* Great-uncle C.C. in *Good-bye, Chicken Little.* It is not surprising, given these circumstances, that the central child character is often a misfit, unhappy, ill-at-ease, depressed. Yet not too much of a misfit; there is no one who is really neurotic in these books. One of their strengths is that it is always possible for the reader to become involved and concerned about what happens to the child. However deprived the background, the reader can usually see something of himself or herself in the characters Betsy Byars creates.

There are certain differences of theme, tone of voice, and structure in the fourteen books between *The Midnight Fox* and *The Animal, The Vegetable, and John D Jones,* but they are small. One of her novels, *Trouble River,* has a historical background, and two of them — only two! — employ a first person narrator *(the Midnight Fox* and *The Winged Colt of Casa Mia),* a device Betsy Byars does not handle well. *The Winged Colt of Casa Mia* also happens to be her sole work of fantasy, a medium in which she is not really skillful. It is the realistic, everyday, humdrum details of ordinary existence that show her at her best; some of her finest writing concerns children doing simple, indeed silly little things just to pass the time — Sara dyeing her sneakers in *The Summer of the Swans,* the Monopoly game that lasted a day and a half in *After the Goat Man,* and, in *The Midnight Fox:*

Petie was transferring the ant from one sneaker to the other, crossing his legs all kinds of different ways, so that no matter which way the ant ran he was always on the sneaker. This ant must have thought, Wow! There are one thousand boys lined up here and I will never get to the end of them.

However, despite her success as a writer of realistic fiction, some of her stories are marred by improbability. *The Eighteenth Emergency* is one of her most popular and most widely read books, but it is one of the least convincing, a short story spun out to novella length, with characterization that is really caricature: Mouse Fawley's fear of almost everything doesn't sound genuinely felt — the language and concepts of the seventeen emergencies are too unreal, too amusing — and his acceptance of being beaten up as a matter of honor does not ring true. He does not, in fact, owe a debt of honor — Marv, a junior version of The Incredible Hulk, may well be annoyed that Mouse has written "Marv Hammerman" under a picture of Neanderthal Man, but hitting Mouse until the blood flows is not, by any standards except those of revenge justice, a way of retaliation the reader should be asked to approve. Lennie, the main character of *The TV Kid*, seems to be cured of his mindless addiction to television by being bitten by a rattlesnake; the book appears to be saying that some violent external shock, such as a snakebite, can jolt a withdrawn unhappy child into the world of reality. Temporarily, of course, it could do so — Betsy Byars's portrayal of the pain that absorbs Lennie's whole attention is well done, and moving; but it does not prove that the sudden conversion is permanent, though that is implied. Betsy Byars clearly dislikes television. In several of her books, attention is drawn to the cheap escapism and the lack of intelligent content of many children's programs, and to the vulgar banality of most commercials. In particular, she seems — rightly — to be bothered by the negative effect of a great deal of television watching on the development of children's minds and imaginations. One applauds this, and though other authors, such as M. E. Kerr in *I'll Love You When You're More Like Me* have made similar statements, Betsy Byars is perhaps alone in making television addiction the main theme of a story. Yet in *The TV Kid* her moral concern is too obtrusive; the book is spoiled by the narrative being manipulated to illustrate a point. *The Cartoonist* should have been her masterpiece: only in *The Night Swimmers* is her humor so amusing, her observation so sharp, her ability to make the reader sympathize with one character and despise another so effective. But it is marred by the way the narrative develops. Alfie has locked himself in his room, an attic, and he refuses to come out; his brother and sister-in-law have been told they can move in there and he is very resentful. His mother threatens to call the fire department, but her daughter, Alma, says he has got to come down by himself; there are things she has had to accept and work out by herself, and that is what Alfie must do. This seemingly intractable problem, however, is solved not by Alfie, but by the expedient of the brother and the sister-in-law deciding *not* to move into the attic. It is all too easy, therefore, for Alfie to come out. The conclusion of this otherwise exceptionally fine novel — a witty, humane, absorbing story — is a rather lame anticlimax.

Betsy Byars is particularly good at opening sentences, first paragraphs, first chapters. *The Night Swimmers* begins with this sentence:

> When the swimming pool lights were turned out and Colonel and Mrs. Roberts had gone to bed, the Anderson kids came out of the bushes in their underwear.

Not only is this a marvelously rich invitation to read on, but it is a powerful image that seems to dominate the book. A strong, central, visual image often leaves a vivid impression on Betsy Byars's readers — Grandma, in *Trouble River*, shooting the rapids, sitting in a rocking chair perched on the middle of a raft, is one example, despite the resonances it has with more than one rapid-shooting movie; Grandfather in *After the Goat Man*, alone in his cabin, defying the builders of the new freeway is another; Sammy and his grandfather in *The House of Wings* staring at each other from opposite ends of a pipe that runs beneath a main road is a third:

> It was a strange sensation. It was as if they were the only two people in the world, staring at each other through the center of the earth.

"The game of Monopoly had been going on for a day and a half" is the opening sentence of *After the Goat Man,* and the first words of *The Animal, The Vegetable, and John D Jones* tell us a great deal about Clara's position in the family —

> Clara sat in the back seat of the Mercedes, staring out the window. In the front seat her father and sister had been having a discussion about television for twenty miles.

The first two pages of *The Pinballs* plunge us immediately into an absorbing, dramatic situation. The day Harvey was to be awarded third prize for writing an essay on "Why I am Proud to be an American," his father, half drunk, "accidentally threw the car into drive instead of reverse. In that wrong gear, he stepped on the gas, ran over Harvey and broke his legs." As a result, Harvey is taken away from his father and put into a foster home. All this before page three! But it is the opening chapter of *The Cartoonist* that is best of all. It is a model first chapter that any would-be writer of the short novel should study; for it establishes, briefly, the outlines of all the main characters, hints at the tensions, the way the plot will develop, suggests where our sympathies are to be withheld, gives a sense of place, social class, and a feeling that this narrative will totally engross the reader. It is all done with great economy — brief, telling phrases and an ironic sense of humor. One would like to quote all eight pages, but two examples will have to suffice. These are the opening words —

> "Alfie?"
> "What?"
> "You studying?"

"Yes," he lied.

"Well, why don't you come down and study in front of the television? It'll take your mind off what you're doing," his mother called.

Of all the adults in Betsy Byars's novels, none is more striking than Alfie's mother — a silly, domineering, emptyheaded, selfish woman who leaves a trail of breakage and unhappiness wherever she goes, a character one would not be surprised to find in a story by M. E. Kerr. Alfie stays up in the attic; he's drawing cartoons, his mother vaguely at the back of his mind in this:

> In the first square of "Super Caterpillar," a giant caterpillar was happily eating New York City. In the second square he was happily eating New York State. In the third he was happily eating the world. In the last square, he was unhappily falling through space, his stomach a big round ball. Alfie was especially pleased with the expression in Super Caterpillar's eyes as he tumbled helplessly through space.

One of the prerequisites of the short novel, if it is to make a strongly effective impression, is the author's ability to be epigrammatic, to be the master of the short phrase or paragraph that says a lot and which will stay in the mind. Betsy Byars is as good in this as M. E. Kerr. When Carlie, in *The Pinballs*, hears that Harvey's father is coming to visit him, she says, "Whoo, next thing you know they'll be letting germs and viruses in." Roy, in *The Night Swimmers*, is a sensitive, anguished child —

> Once in kindergarten he'd accidentally colored his George Washington face mask green and had not been allowed to march in the Parade of Presidents with the other kids. He had waited in the classroom with Miss Penny, weeping with the pain of exile, vowing never to be left out of anything again.

John D, in *The Animal, The Vegetable, and John D Jones* thought of himself as an antidote to the world's new niceness. He saw the world as a great big bland glass of niceness, and he was an acid tablet, dropped in to start things fizzing.

The story of *Good-bye, Chicken Little* is the reaction of Jimmie Little to his Uncle Pete's death. Uncle Pete is an immature, overgrown schoolboy, and he dies, after a drinking bout, walking on a frozen river in answer to a challenge that he dare not cross from one side to the other because the ice might not be safe. The ice cracks; he falls in and is drowned. Jimmie

> felt strange. As soon as his mother had called Uncle Pete a boy, he had found that he himself no longer felt like a boy. He was not a man yet, he knew that, but something vital, something important about boyhood, had been taken away from him with his mother's words. He wasn't sure he would get it back.

Harriet Haywood, in *The Cybil War*, is taunted by the boys about her fatness; she is "a tub of blubber." Her reaction is to push open the door of the girls' restroom "with such force that it swung back and forth five times — a school record." She

> came out of the restroom like a missile. There were two girls with her, and the three of them, in tight formation, seemed like an attack force out of *Star Wars*.

In *The House of Wings* Sammy asks

> "Where's my mom and dad?" His grandfather rocked slowly back and forth like a buoy in the water.
>
> Then his grandfather said one word. "Gone." It was like the sound of an old sad church bell in the hot empty yard. "Gone."

It reminds the reader of James's mother's comment, in Paula Fox's *How Many Miles to Babylon?*, about her missing husband: "Gone, gone, gone." Indeed, the word does sound like "an old sad church bell." Sammy's grandfather tries to explain the importance of all life, human, animal, bird, fish, and wants to convey the reverence he feels but which his grandson lacks. He says —

"They're going to find one dead planet after another, that's what I think. You'll be picking up the newspaper and reading one sorry headline after another. No life on Jupiter. No life on Mars. No life on this planet. No life on that planet. And not until you've seen every one of those headlines, not until you know there's not any life anywhere, *then*, boy, is when you'll know how precious life is."

Animals play an important role in Betsy Byars' work, for there are more than the usual cats and dogs one is likely to find in most children's books, though even these she observes as distinctive creatures. Garbage Dog, in *The Eighteenth Emergency*, is a neglected stray, as timid as the central character. His fears parallel those of Mouse Fawley —

Garbage Dog had not been inside a house for years. He hesitated at the door, and then when Mouse pushed him, he entered. He walked around the edge of the room, avoiding the carpet, until he came to the kitchen. Then he sat uneasily by the table. There was a little hot air blowing on him from under the refrigerator, and this worried him. He moved over by the sink.

"What do you want to eat?" Mouse asked. "Bologna sandwich all right?"

It is, however, wild animals that interest Betsy Byars more than domestic pets. The swans in *The Summer of the Swans* and the goats in *After the Goat Man* act as powerful symbols; the best writing in *The TV Kid* concerns the rattlesnake and the effects of its bite. Horses dominate *The Winged Colt of Casa Mia*, and if they are not as well realized as the menagerie of creatures Grandfather looks after in *The House of Wings*, that is because of the poor quality of the first-person narration. (It is an unusual and interesting device in a children's book to make the first-person narrator an adult, but Betsy Byars does not succeed in portraying Uncle Coot, the sardonic, reclusive ex-Hollywood stunt man, sound totally credible.) The horse, Alado, has wings and can fly like Pegasus; fantastic though that is, it comes over as more plausible than the voice of the main character. Maybe the nephew should have been the narrator — the element of wonder at the fantastic would have sprung naturally from him, particularly as he saw his uncle as a "wonder," not unlike the flying horse in his feats of daring as a stunt man. The portrayal of the fox in *The Midnight Fox* is excellent — as physically real as the fox in *The Iron Giant* by Ted Hughes —

> Her steps as she crossed the field were lighter and quicker than a cat's. As she came closer I could see that her black fur was tipped with white. It was as if it were midnight and the moon were shining on her fur, frosting it. The wind parted her fur as it changed directions. Suddenly she stopped. She was ten feet away now, and with the changing of the wind she had got my scent. She looked right at me.

The description is accurate, detailed, vivid, and the words "as if it were midnight and the moon were shining on her fur" is illuminating, the one needed touch of poetry. *The House of Wings* has several good passages describing birds. Grandfather and the wounded blind crane, observed together by Sammy, make a strange duo —

> Then gently he lifted the bird against his side. The tips of his white elbows were as sharp as knives, and the crane's stick legs ran, scissors-like, in the air for a moment. It was a picture of sharp and impossible angles.

The repeated "i" sounds of "lifted," "tips," "stick," "scissors," "picture" well emphasize the "sharp and impossible angles." In the same story, the raccoon asleep in the middle of the bed after eating five jars of jelly, and the owl who fell down a chimney and was discovered next morning in the stove's ashes, are anecdotes related with simplicity and a sense of wonder. The owl is beautifully observed:

> The owl made a faint hissing sound, like steam escaping. Then he swooped down into the tub and pounced

on the grasshopper with both feet. His talons curled around the grasshopper, and he put it in his mouth . . . Then suddenly Sammy noticed how intently the owl was staring at him. He took a step backward. He said quickly, "That was the only one I could find." He backed out into the hall and went quietly down the stairs.

This time it is the verbs that make this effective — "swooped," "pounced," and "curled" contrasting with "put" and "intently . . . staring;" then Sammy's movements — "took a step backward," "backed out," "went quietly." Betsy Byars's writing at its best is as fine as that of the great stylists of contemporary children's authors — Philippa Pearce, Paula Fox, Lucy Boston. The material from which she makes a children's novel is often similar to the material M. E. Kerr uses in a young adult novel, but she is the better *writer* of the two.

She is, as I said, a good observer of the trivia children concern themselves with; she is also effective in portraying the fantasies that go through their heads, and their memories of extraordinary situations. Harold, in *After the Goat Man*, cannot forget that when he was six the kids in his class put on a Noah's Ark play; the pairs had all been chosen, so he had to be an extra hippopotamus. (He is a very fat boy.)

> In his dreams all the other animals had clomped happily into the ark. The heavy wooden door had slammed shut. The extra hippopotamus had been left alone.

Tommy, in *The Midnight Fox*, feels adults always seem to worry about the wrong things —

> One time Petie Burkis's sitter came out and Petie was stuck up in this tree, about to fall, and she said, "Petie, come down out of that wind — you're going to get earache!" Petie made up a headline about it — BOY BREAKS TWENTY-SEVEN BONES — AVOIDS EARACHE.

Mouse Fawley's seventeen ludicrous emergencies are another example of a child's fantasies; so are Harvey's lists, in *The Pinballs*, of the awful things that have happened to him; and, in *The TV Kid*, Lennie imagining himself to be a winning contestant in a television quiz show. John D in *The Animal, The Vegetable, and John D Jones* is writing a series of books with titles like "You Are Smarter Than Your Teachers." Alfie, in *The Cartoonist*, has his comic strips, and Harold, in *After the Goat Man*, his self-important visions of himself as a TV or radio announcer. All these situations are seen as amusing, and hopefully temporary — necessary stages a child may have to go through before he can cope with the real world.

The material of *The Pinballs* is uncannily similar to that of *The Great Gilly Hopkins* by Katherine Paterson, though, as both books were published within a year of each other, it is unlikely that either writer knew what the other was doing. (*The Pinballs*, in fact, preceded *The Great Gilly Hopkins*.) Harvey, Thomas J., and Carlie live in a foster home — Thomas J. because he has no parents; Harvey and Carlie because their home situations are so intolerable that they have been removed by order of the courts. Mrs. Mason, their foster mother, is not the larger-than-life figure of Mame Trotter in *The Great Gilly Hopkins*; she is somewhat colorless — but nevertheless almost as saintly. The chief parallel between the two books is in the characters of Carlie and Gilly — both of them mixtures of toughness and insecurity, never at a loss for an answer, and both commanding a wide vocabulary of wit and repartee. However, Carlie is no more of a successful creation than Gilly Hopkins. She is, we are told,

> hard as a coconut. She never said anything polite. When anyone asked her how she was, she answered, "What's it to you?" or "Bug off."

But, in fact, like Gilly Hopkins, she is generous, compassionate, not a desperate problem.

Neither character comes over to the reader as the author wants us to see her. The trouble is that the authors fight

43

shy of portraying the real nature of many kids who find themselves in foster homes, perhaps because some adults would object to such material. Writers of teenage novels avoid the depiction of adolescent sexuality for similar reasons. In answer to the question, how real do you want your realism? Mr. and Mrs. Average Parent, Librarian, and Teacher would say, of children's books and young adult books, not too absolutely real. Alas! — for the kids frequently have a different answer.

The Summer of the Swans and *The Night Swimmers* are probably Betsy Byars's finest books. *The Summer of the Swans* has an exciting well-paced narrative, as good as that of *The Cartoonist,* but it does not depend on a *convenient* chance for its outcome; chance, yes — but one that is more likely than that of Bubba and Maureen simply changing their minds about living in Alfie's attic. It is the story of the summer Sara Godfrey finds all the certainties of childhood no longer certainties; in particular, the story of the day her mentally retarded brother disappears. Much of the plot is concerned with the search for him. Sara finds him, by chance — but it is plausible, for it is very likely that Charlie has not strayed far. For Sara, finding Charlie restores at least one of the certainties she thought she had lost. Looking after Charlie had become a nuisance; it stopped her fully enjoying herself with her friends, but when she faces the awful possibility that her brother might be dead, or at least badly injured, she realizes how much she loves him, how necessary he is to her existence. And if the other certainty she would like to restore to her family — the return of her father — does not happen, she advances a step towards maturity in finding her first boy friend, Joe Melby — someone she thought she had always despised. Characterization in this novel is excellent — not only Sara herself, but her elder sister Wanda (this relationship is exceptionally well done; tense and quarrelsome, but also affectionate and important), eccentric Aunt Willie, Sara's best friend Mary, Charlie, ineffectual Dad. The dialogue, too, never falters. *The Summer of the Swans* thoroughly deserved the Newbery Medal it was awarded in 1971.

"So much happens here, so simply, in the taut space of a few summer days, that every word and gesture has to count," said *The School Library Journal* review of *The Night Swimmers*: an accurate assessment, for though this novel is as brief as most others written by Betsy Byars, it is perhaps the most complex. The Anderson children have no mother; their father is a second-rate Country and Western singer — he once made the number thirty-seven position on the charts — and he is usually away from home at night. Retta, the eldest child, has to cook, keep house, and act as surrogate mother to her two brothers. She is bossy, unbending and wilful, but genuinely concerned that Roy and Johnny should be happy. She wants them to love her. Johnny, however, grows to hate her, particularly when she tries to stop him — because she is jealous — from forming a friendship outside the family; and she really does not know how to cope with Roy, who is dependent and vulnerable. At the climax of the book Roy nearly drowns while Retta is arguing with Johnny; this brings the family situation to the attention of adults outside the family. The story concludes with their father realizing that he has more responsibilities to his children than he had thought, but it is no conventional happy ending. The insights in this book are memorable; the words have a forceful bluntness that is as striking as the language in *The Cartoonist*. Retta "felt as bewildered as a child whose dolls have come to life and are demanding real care and attention;" "the unswallowed, unspoken pain of her mother's death stayed in her throat so long that sometimes she thought she would die of it," and —

> She had suddenly felt as if she were seeing her father so clearly that her image of him might be damaged forever, the way one's eyes are damaged by looking directly at the sun.

The Night Swimmers is a somber and powerful achievement.

In the realistic novel for children and young adults that delineates the everyday events of school and home, the pleasures and pains of parent-child relationships — and those with brothers, sisters, friends — contemporary American writers have produced a much more impressive body of work than the British. Between them, Betsy Byars and M. E. Kerr leave their rivals, both British *and* American, far behind. Their main strengths are in focusing on the importance of adults to teenagers and children, in portraying relationships with wit, subtlety and complexity, and — particularly Betsy Byars — in achieving the goal of high literary excellence.

References

BETSY BYARS
The Midnight Fox Viking 1968; Faber 1970
Trouble River Viking 1969
The Summer of the Swans Viking 1970; Hippo Books 1980
The House of Wings Viking 1972; Bodley Head 1973
The Eighteenth Emergency Viking 1973; Bodley Head 1974
The Winged Colt of Casa Mia Viking 1973
After the Goat Man Viking 1974; Bodley Head 1975
The TV Kid Viking 1976; Bodley Head 1976
The Pinballs Harper 1977; Bodley Head 1977
The Cartoonist Viking 1978; Bodley Head 1978
Good-bye, Chicken Little Harper 1979; Bodley Head 1979
The Night Swimmers Delacorte 1980; Bodley Head 1980
The Cybil War Viking 1981; Bodley Head 1981
The Animal, The Vegetable, and John D Jones Delacorte 1982
PAULA FOX
How Many Miles to Babylon? David White 1967; Macmillan, London, 1968
TED HUGHES
The Iron Man Faber 1968; in America, as *The Iron Giant* Harper 1968
M. E. KERR
Is That You, Miss Blue? Harper 1975
I'll Love You When You're More Like Me Harper 1977
KATHERINE PATERSON
The Great Gilly Hopkins Crowell 1978; Gollancz 1979

Hospitals Where We Heal

TED HUGHES

Ted Hughes is generally recognized in the English-speaking world as one of the most important poets of the second half of the twentieth century, but his achievements as a writer for children are not so widely known. In his writing for young people he shows himself to be a jack-of-all-trades, though I would *not* add a master of none: He has produced volumes of poetry specifically for children, the text of a picture book, short stories, the unclassifiable *The Iron Giant* (a modern morality-cum-myth), one major critical essay, four plays, and a book on creative writing. A full-length novel is the only form he has eschewed so far. He has an immense concern for the young, for their vulnerability in a dangerous, industrialized world; he seems in this to be as much a teacher as a creative artist: the driving forces behind his writing are the need to stimulate creativity and imagination in children and to encourage the right kind of education to counteract the evils — as he sees it — of a blind faith in scientific progress. In this he resembles nineteenth-century children's authors more than those of our own time; though never overtly didactic, he is certainly a moralist (and on occasion a stern moralist) — someone who feels that the young are *not* best left to their own devices, but need to be guided and taught. This may sound unfashionable, indeed to some reprehensible, but it has never impeded his creative powers. He does not believe, as a Victorian author might, that books should frighten the young reader into being good or should offer soft, sentimental solutions, but he does believe that children's fiction should not turn its back — as it sometimes does — on modern technology and wallow nostalgically in a cozy, rural past.

He feels with some passion that children's literature is more important now than it has ever been, particularly as a corrective to scientific discovery and so-called advance.

The poetry need not detain us long, though six of his ten books for children are collections of verse. They are, curiously, much less successful than the plays and the stories. Or maybe it is not so curious: his energies as a poet have chiefly gone into the succession of volumes from *The Hawk in the Rain* to *Moortown*, major works for the adult reader. In writing verse for children he often seems to be floundering. The irony and grim humor is missing (though it is there in the prose) and is replaced by a childlike dottiness that is in effect child*ish*:

> "They are taking me to the Queen," thinks Nessie,
> "And the Duke of Edinburgh will say 'There's a Bonnie
>   Lassie!'
> "Then I shall be all right, I shall have class,
> "And everybody will say 'Oh everybody knows Nessie,
>   she's a grand lass.'
> "And all these good people are bringing this to pass."
>   *(Nessie the Mannerless Monster)*

The themes are often similar to those of the adult poetry — landscape, usually bleak and without the presence of man, and animals. The volume called *Season Songs* is almost entirely about landscape and weather, and though it contains some remarkable lines and images, some startling and original perceptions —

> There came this day and he was autumn.
> His mouth was wide
> And red as a sunset.
> His tail was an icicle.
>   ("There Came a Day")

or

> The first sorrow of autumn
> Is the slow goodbye
> Of the garden who stands so long in the evening
> A brown poppy head,

48

The stalk of a lily,
And still cannot go.
　　　("The Seven Sorrows")
— there is an unsureness, particularly when he uses rhyme:

But the cod is in the tide-rip
　　Like a key in a purse.
The deer are on the bare-blown hill
　　Like smiles on a nurse.
　　　("The Warm and the Cold")

In his adult poetry Ted Hughes rarely, if ever, uses rhyme: perhaps he feels it adds little to the structure of a stanza. It is odd that in writing for children he frequently uses rhyme, and rarely with success; it is an obstacle with which he seems to collide, gracelessly.

Ted Hughes's finest poems are about animals: perhaps no one has ever written so much on this subject and so well. Animals, real and invented, abound in the verse for children. In *Under the North Star* there are memorable phrases and descriptions — the black bear's comment about himself, "I am God's clown"; clams in winter "gasped with blue cold"; the woodpecker is "rubber-necked"; "the goofy Moose is "the walking house-frame"; the wolf "licks the world clean as a plate/ And leaves his own bones." But often these poems sound like simplifications of the animal poems in the adult books, or footnotes to them, not completely new ideas. There is also uncertainty in the nonsense verse of *Meet My Folks!* The imagination behind these poems is splendid — a sister who is actually a crow pretending to be a human, a father whose job is inspecting holes, a grandmother who knits clothes for wasps and goldfish, an aunt who grows man-eating thistles — but the use of rhyme is a hit-and-miss affair:

The very thought makes me iller and iller
Bert's brought home a gigantic Gorilla!
　　　("My Brother Bert")

works well; it's outrageous and funny, but

Not to forget the Bandicoot

> Who would certaintly peer from his battered old boot
> ("My Brother Bert")

does not work: not only does the second line contain too many words, but a boot — as opposed to anything else — is the bandicoot's home only because the poet needs a rhyme.

Ted Hughes has not yet found a proper voice for himself as a poet for children, excellent though some individual poems may be. He probably needs to move away completely from the themes of his adult poetry and forge an entirely different instrument for what he wants to say.

Poetry in the Making is the printed version of a series of talks he gave on BBC Radio for the schools program, *Listening and Writing*. In the introduction to the book, he says that nothing, except for the odd word, has been changed; and indeed the prose throughout has the sound of someone speaking. Each of the eleven talks is an attempt to motivate young people to write, poetry in particular, although two sections are devoted to the novel. There is much of autobiographical interest here, for Ted Hughes tells us how and why he started, in his mid-teens, to write, and he gives the reader much absorbing background detail about the genesis of some of his best-known poems — for instance, "Pike," "Wind," and "The Thought-Fox." His advice to young people is exemplary: he is enthusiastic, helpful, never condescending, and always practical. Words, he says, that are important are "those which we hear, like 'click' or 'chuckle,' or which we see, like 'freckled' or 'veined' . . . words which belong directly to one of the five senses. Or words which act and seem to use their muscles, like 'flick' or 'balance.' " Most words, he adds, "belong to several of the senses at once, as if each one had eyes, ears and tongue, or ears and fingers and a body to move with." Do not worry at first about punctuation, but "keep your eyes, your ears, your nose, your taste, your touch, your whole being on the thing you are turning into words." *Poetry in the Making* reflects many of the orthodox ideas about teaching English that were current at the time it was written, the late sixties —

creativity and originality at almost any cost: teaching English has changed since then, but Ted Hughes's concern that children should enjoy writing, and the immense experience that he is able to impart, mean that the book rarely has a dated, passé feeling to it. Reading *Poetry in the Making* is a fascinating experience, for writers do not often allow us to peep so much behind the scenes as he does, to glimpse so much of the processes of creation: maybe that is because many of them are not so conscious of what they are doing as he is.

The four short plays in the volume *The Coming of the Kings* were also written for children's radio programs. Two of them, *Beauty and the Beast* and *Sean, the Fool, the Devil and the Cats*, are variants on ancient folk tales; *The Tiger's Bones* is a surrealistic fantasy about a mad scientist who thinks the end of the world is coming; and the best, *The Coming of the Kings*, is a nativity play. It is extremely difficult to write a nativity play and avoid the pitfalls of cliché and mawkishness; most modern versions of the Christmas story do not. A magnificent exception is *The Business of Good Government* by John Arden. *The Coming of the Kings* does not have the luminous, simple beauty of John Arden's dialogue, but it is a thoughtful and amusing piece, well within the capabilities of the child actor. John Arden and Ted Hughes succeed — where others do not — because they shift the focus of attention away from the traditional central characters to less important people; in *The Business of Good Government* the principal figure is Herod; in *The Coming of the Kings* it is two people who are not mentioned in the Bible, but who must have been in Bethlehem on that night — the innkeeper and his wife. However, effective though these four plays are, they are minor works, the products of a writer who is simply enjoying himself in a role that is not usually his own, and finding out whether he can do it or not.

How the Whale Became, a collection of eleven short stories, and *The Iron Giant* which, though it is subtitled "a story in five nights," is a continuous narrative, are Ted

Hughes's two works of prose fiction for children. The first of these is flawless, but does not aim at anything very profound, whereas *The Iron Giant* is on an altogether different level. *How the Whale Became* takes its central idea from the *Just So Stories* of Rudyard Kipling; each chapter relates, in a fantastic and humorous way, how a particular animal obtained its shape or size or coloring or behavior. The fox and the dog both applied to Man to be the guardian of the farm, but the fox couldn't stop eating the hens so he had to be banished; the hare leaps and rushes and acts in such an apparently crazed manner because he is in love with the moon and is always chasing after her; the polar bear lives in the Arctic because she's extremely vain, and loves to use the icebergs as mirrors in which she can admire herself. The best story is how the tortoise became. It had no shell at first and was the fastest of animals, the great athlete, but the other creatures shunned it: it had no skin. So God made it a skin:

"I would like," said Torto, "a skin that I can put on, or take off, whenever I please."

God frowned.

"I'm afraid," he said, "I have none like that."

"Then make one," replied Torto. "You're God."

God went away and came back within an hour.

"Do you want a beautiful skin?" he asked. "Or do you mind if it's very ugly?"

"I don't care what sort of a skin it is," said Torto, "so long as I can take it off and put it back on again whenever I please."

God went away again, and again came back within an hour.

"Here it is. That's the best I can do."

"What's this!" cried Torto. "But it's horrible!"

"Take it or leave it," said God, and walked away. Torto examined the skin. It was tough, rough, and stiff.

"It's like a coconut," he said. "With holes in it."

And so it was. Only it was shiny. When he tried it on, he found it quite snug. It had only one disadvantage. He could move only very slowly in it.

God plays an interesting role, not unlike the God of medieval moralities and mystery plays: he is portrayed as a kindly human being, capable of making mistakes — a nice touch, when one thinks of evolutionary "mistakes" that have occurred — and he is not always sure of what to do next. The whale, for example, was originally a plant that mysteriously appeared in God's garden; each day its size doubled, so that the garden was ruined, the walls smashed, the road outside blocked. It was on the advice of the other animals that God pulled it up and threw it over a cliff, for only in the sea was there room enough for it.

The invention in *How the Whale Became* is ingenious and amusing throughout, the prose sure-footed and simple without being dull:

> When God made a creature, he first of all shaped it in clay. Then he baked it in the oven of the sun until it was hard. Then he took it out of the oven and, when it was cool, breathed life into it. Last of all, he pulled its skin on to it like a tight jersey.
>
> All the animals got different skins. If it was a cold day, God would give to the animals he made on that day a dense, woolly skin. Snow was falling heavily when he made the sheep and the bears.
>
> If it was a hot day, the new animals got a thin skin. On the day he made greyhounds and dachshunds and boys and girls, the weather was so hot God had to wear a sun hat and was calling endlessly for iced drinks.

The Iron Giant, though it began as stories Ted Hughes improvised for his own children, has an altogether more serious purpose. It is an attempt to create a myth-like tale that takes into account the world of modern technology, something the author feels has been ignored by contemporary children's authors. In "Myth and Education" he says that the early education of students he used to teach completely neglected the real major experience of their lives, namely the collision with the American technological world, and, beyond that, the opening up, by physics and so on, of a universe which was completely uninhabited except by atoms and the energy of atoms . . . What they should have been taught was a mythology where all these things would have had a place and meaningful relationships one with another, the student, the technology and the chaos, and his terror of the chaos.

So when I began to tell this following story to my own children later, I shaped it in a particular way.

A gigantic iron monster suddenly appears on the top of a cliff (no explanation is given for this); he falls over the edge and is smashed to pieces. But he fits himself together, walks inland and begins to eat up all the farm machinery he can find. The farmers are terrified and dig a vast pit to trap him; a small boy called Hogarth lures him into the pit, which is then filled up with earth so that the giant is buried. But he gets out, and on Hogarth's instigation, he is taken to a scrapyard where he lives contentedly on rusty gas stoves and old cars. Another monster — "terribly black, terribly scaly, terribly knobbly, terribly horned, terribly hairy, terribly clawed, terribly fanged" — from outer space then lands on Australia, and threatens to destroy whole countries if it isn't fed. The iron giant challenges it to a duel of strength and wins. The space monster is now his slave and is sent off to create the music of the spheres, which makes everyone so happy that there is peace on earth ever after.

One can recognize in this story not only a belief that modern technology should be used for man's benefits rather than for destructive purposes, but also a number of themes found in ancient myth — the death of a god, resurrection, the duel or jousting between the hero and the villain, the struggle between good and evil. The view of the world, however, is not Manichean, as is so often the case in myth; Ted Hughes departs from tradition when his story suggests that evil exists in all of us and has to be recognized for what it is; that only then can it be tamed and used for good. In "Myth and Education" he says he was attempting, in *The Iron Giant*, to create something that was opposite to the legend of St. George and the dragon in which evil is destroyed; that sort of tale "sets up as an ideal pattern for any dealing with unpleasant or irrational experience the complete suppression of the terror . . . It is the symbolic story of creating a neurosis." The argument, in both *The Iron Giant* itself, and in the author's own comments in "Myth and Education," is powerful and convincing.

The child reader, of course, is not going to be aware of all this, at least not in terms that can be verbalized in this way; but he will undoubtedly absorb in a subconscious fashion what is being said. Every story we tell a child "is a whole kit of blueprints for dealing with himself and for dealing with his own imagination," Ted Hughes says in "Myth and Education." And *The Iron Giant* is a story that is told most seductively. The virtues of his finest poetry are all present in its prose: as, the ability to create landscape in a few telling words — "Just before dawn, as the darkness grew blue and the shapes of the rocks separated from each other, two seagulls flew crying over the rocks"; and emotional tension:

> Suddenly he felt a strange feeling. He felt he was being watched. He felt afraid. He turned and looked up the steep field to the top of the high cliff. Behind that skyline was the sheer rocky cliff and the sea. And on that skyline, just above the edge of it, in the dusk, were two green lights. What were two green lights doing at the top of the cliff?
>
> Then, as Hogarth watched, a huge dark figure climbed up over the cliff top. The two lights rose into the sky. They were the giant figure's eyes. A giant black figure, taller than a house, black and towering in the twilight, with green headlight eyes. The Iron Giant! There he stood on the cliff top, looking inland.

The frightening size of the giant is emphasized in a number of effective similes — "taller than a house", "his chest was as big as a cattle truck", "the great iron head, square like a bedroom" — but he seems a dwarf when the monster arrives from outer space. The "vast, indescribable, terrible" eyes of the space-bat-angel-dragon were "each one as big as Switzerland" and it sat "covering the whole of Australia, its tail trailing away over Tasmania into the sea, its foreclaws on the headlands of the Gulf of Carpentaria." The contrast between the two monsters is neatly illustrated by what they eat. The iron giant eats old trucks and rusty gas stoves — harmless, indeed useful. But the space-bat-angel-dragon demands

> . . . living things. People, animals, forests, it didn't care which, so long as the food was alive. But it had better be fed quickly; otherwise, it would roll out its tongue longer than the Trans-Siberian railway and lick huge swathes of life off the surface of the earth — cities, forests, farmlands, whatever there was. It would leave the world looking like a charred pebble. . . .

The iron giant represents twentieth-century technology, tamed and in the service of mankind; the space-bat-angel-dragon is the untamed, horrifying energies of space.

Another quality of the writing is the humor, a bit grim compared with *How the Whale Became*, but entertaining nonetheless. When the space-bat-angel-dragon lands "it knocked down certain skyscrapers, sent tidal waves sweeping into harbors, and threw herds of cows on to their backs. All over the world, anybody who happened to be riding a bicycle at that moment instantly fell off." And the author never neglects the small detail the very young reader always likes, even if it is not particularly relevant. A family of holiday-makers is having a picnic right over the spot — though they do not know it — where the iron giant is buried; it is the moment when the giant chooses to reappear, but Ted Hughes has time to tell us what they were eating: "a plate of sandwiches, a big pie, a roasted chicken, a bottle of milk, a bowl of tomatoes, a bagful of boiled eggs, a dish of butter and a loaf of bread, with cheese and salt."

The Iron Giant is not without defects. Hogarth is a bit too clever to be totally credible, and the space-bat-angel-dragon is not as convincing a monster as the iron giant. He does not appear until the penultimate chapter, and, because he is such an important figure, the narrative seems to shift direction, leaving the reader with the impression that he could have been tacked on as an afterthought, to give the story the required climax and conclusion, rather than being part of the author's ideas from the beginning. The contest between the monsters is too heavily loaded in the iron giant's favor: in fact, the last two chapters are not as well thought out as the first three, even if they illustrate perfectly Ted Hughes's ideas about harnessing the "evil" of technology for the benefit of mankind. But imperfect though it may be, *The Iron Giant* is remarkable for its originality, its writing virtues, and its attempt to place modern technology at the center of a children's story that also retains the age-old characteristics of myth.

"Myth and Education," originally a paper given at the 1969 Exeter Conference on children's fiction and subsequently published in *Children's literature in education,* is not just a commentary on *The Iron Giant.* It is, in my opinion, one of the most interesting critical documents on children's literature of recent years. It is not invariably in book form or in the published essay that good criticism first emerges; in the past two decades much that is worthwhile began — and this is particularly true of contributions by the authors themselves — as a talk at a book conference. Catherine Storr's "Fear and Evil in Children's Books" and Penelope Lively's "Children and Memory" are milestones in contemporary criticism, and both essays, too, were originally talks given at a book conference. In "Myth and Education" Ted Hughes questions some of the fundamental assumptions of modern education, the so-called "enlightenment" of the past three hundred years, and points to what he calls "the breakdown of all negotiations between our scientific mental attitude and our inner life." Modern education with its tremendous bias towards science and technology, he says, began

> by questioning superstitions and ended by prohibiting imagination itself as a reliable mental faculty, branding it more or less as a criminal in a scientific society . . . The scientific attitude, which is the crystallization of the rational attitude, has to be passive in face of the facts if it is to record the facts accurately . . . This detached, inwardly inert objectivity has become the prevailing mental attitude of our time. It is taught in schools as an ideal. The result is something resembling mental paralysis. It can be seen in every corner of our life.

This is obviously an extreme point of view, an almost savage attack on the harm done to us by technology. Photography and television come in for a bashing — "OK for scientists," Ted Hughes suggests, "but disastrous for human beings in general." He looks wistfully over his shoulder at Platonic ideas — the creation in children of an imagination by stories, folk tales and myths — but admits that even in Plato's Greece it was never more than a proposal. In a technological civilization, he says, literature is even more important than in ancient times; its imaginative importance is paramount. He is marvelously persuasive about the effect that literature has, particularly on young minds. Imaginative stimulus, he argues, can have enormous consequences; a child absorbed in a story is like someone in a trance: "whatever happens to him in the story happens under conditions of hypnosis. In other words, it really happens. If in a story he is put through a humiliating defeat, the effects on him are of real defeat." It is the same for adults:

> We can't ignore that when we read a story, and enter it in a completely imaginative way, the story works on all parts of our nature, and it's impossible to know finally what its influences are . . . This is the appeal of great works of imaginative literature to us as adults,

that they are hospitals where we heal, where our imaginations are healed, that when they are evil works they are also battlefields where we get injured.

We have, therefore, an immense obligation to give our children the right kind of literature.

Ted Hughes does not specify what the right kind of literature should be; he gives us no examples. That is not necessary; we, his readers, are probably better as judges for having our minds so stimulated by such a polemic as "Myth and Education." For it fulfills one of the major functions of criticism: it makes the reader go away and *think*, forces him to question his assumptions and look at literature with new eyes. To find a list of recommended books tacked on to such an essay would be shallow; Ted Hughes knows perfectly well that his opinions here are no more *ex cathedra* than those of anyone else. To return to basics, as he does, is much more important than saying, for instance, that *Charlotte's Web* is a good book for children if they want to come to terms with death, useful though that information may be. His own fallibility is neatly illustrated by his review, in *Children's literature in education*, of *The God Beneath the Sea*, a rewriting by Edward Blishen and Leon Garfield of some of the Greek myths with illustrations by Charles Keeping; placed beside Alan Garner's incisive and outspoken comments — "The Death of Myth" — on the same book in the same journal, Ted Hughes's piece seems woolly and superficial, giving us little idea of the virtues and defects of the work in question, a task Alan Garner accomplishes admirably.

So the most interesting and successful writing for and about children by one of the finest of modern poets is in prose. In his poetry for children Ted Hughes seems to feel the need to simplify his concepts and vocabulary, instead of making the reader stretch; the result is that at times he is uneasy, or shrill, or trite, or unfunny when he has wanted to be humorous. In the prose, the "great poet" image does not intrude. He begins with a clean sheet, no previous achievements to disturb him, and therefore in *How the Whale Became* and *The Iron Giant* the tone of voice is assured; the humor makes us laugh, and nothing seems banal or strained. In "Myth and Education" he is able to think and argue with feeling and intelligence. His poetry for adults is sometimes criticized for its narrowness of range, but the variety in his work for children is remarkable: one can only wish he could find more time to write for the young, particularly in prose.

References

TED HUGHES

    The Hawk in the Rain Faber 1957; Harper 1957
    Meet My Folks! Faber 1961; Bobbs n.d.
    How the Whale Became Faber 1963; Atheneum 1964
    Nessie the Mannerless Monster Faber 1964; in America as *Nessie the Monster* Bobbs-Merrill 1974
    Poetry in the Making Faber 1967; in America as *Poetry Is* Doubleday 1970
    The Iron Man Faber 1968; in America as *The Iron Giant* Harper 1968
    "Myth and Education" in *Children's literature in education*, March 1970
    Review of *The God Beneath the Sea*, in *Children's literature in education*, November 1970
    The Coming of the Kings Faber 1970; in America as *The Tiger's Bones and Other Plays for Children* Viking 1974
    Season Songs Faber 1976; Viking 1976
    Moortown Faber 1979; Harper 1979
    Under the North Star Faber 1981; Viking 1981

JOHN ARDEN

    The Business of Good Government Methuen 1963; Grove 1966

EDWARD BLISHEN and LEON GARFIELD

    The God Beneath the Sea Longman 1970; Pantheon 1971

ALAN GARNER

    "The Death of Myth" in *Children's literature in education*, November 1970

RUDYARD KIPLING

    Just So Stories first published in 1902

PENELOPE LIVELY
"Children and Memory" in *The Horn Book Magazine*, August
1973

CATHERINE STORR
"Fear and Evil in Children's Books" in *Children's literature in
education*, March 1970

E. B. WHITE
Charlotte's Web Harper 1952; Hamish Hamilton 1952

There's No Such Thing As Fairness

Jan Mark

Few first novels have achieved such acclaim as Jan Mark's *Thunder and Lightnings*. It was the winner of the Penguin/ Guardian competition; it was awarded the 1976 Carnegie Medal, and it was lavishly praised by critics and reviewers. It is a remarkable book in many ways, but its huge critical success has ultimately done its writer a disservice by helping to obscure the very considerable merits of the rest of her work. One view of Jan Mark's novels, as expressed by Peter Hunt in his essay "Whatever Happened to Jan Mark?", suggests that her progress has been downhill all the way, a descent into fashionable obscurity of meaning; that spontaneous, genuinely felt life has been edged out of her writing by contrived, conventional plots; that, somehow, winning the prizes turned her head and made her produce smart, pseudo-clever novels beloved only by some in-group of children's book people. This view of Jan Mark seems to me to be wholly wrong, and particularly irritating is the idea that winning literary awards is likely to divert an author of integrity from what he or she really should be doing. Robert Westall wrote, in 1979, that winning the Carnegie made *him* write "books for the children of publishers, librarians and the literary gent of The Times," and while this may well be a truthful statement about the stories that he wrote for a period following *The Machine-Gunners*, he is probably quite exceptional in having been influenced in such a manner. His comment is not valid as far as Jan Mark or other Carnegie winners are concerned.

The assessment by Peter Hunt of Jan Mark's books is a rather long-winded way of asking why she did not write another novel just like *Thunder and Lightnings* — a common enough complaint by readers of a book they have thoroughly enjoyed, who are disappointed to find that other stories by the same author do not encapsulate them in the same world. In fact, *Thunder and Lightnings* is unique; any attempt to repeat it would be disastrous. The development of the slightly uneasy friendship between the two central characters, Andrew and Victor, is beautifully done — the joyous surface of the book masks the underlying tensions and complexities, so that the reader is aware only at certain points that its theme is, to quote Andrew's mother —

> There's no such thing as fairness. It's a word made up to keep children quiet. When you discover it's a fraud, then you're starting to grow up.

That life is very often an unjust, unpleasant and bloody battleground, a struggle for the survival of the fittest, is the theme of all Jan Mark's novels; but in *Thunder and Lightnings* it is on the whole buried beneath a very rich texture of incident, anecdote, and detail about two contrasting households, school life, the patterns of living in rural Norfolk, aircraft, comic dialogue and characters, and some very evocative writing that varies from the poetic and sensuous to the amusingly grotesque:

> The house was long and low, lurking behind the bushes with its head down.

> At once, the little sound changed to a furious roar, so suddenly that he half expected to see the sky crazed all over like a cracked bowl.

> Bob had the kind of moustache that parrots could perch on and rarely said anything other than "Bang on!"

> "Yes, but that's not right to spoil a funeral," said Victor. "After all, that's the last party you ever have."

Thunder and Lightnings is an unusual book in that it is almost entirely without a plot; an extreme example, in fact, of a story that has no recognizable beginning, middle, and end. Its apparently disconnected events are a way, in fact, of showing the development of the friendship between Victor and Andrew, and the recurring motifs — the guinea-pigs, for instance, or Victor's attempts to draw, and, above all, the airplanes — are not only realistic details of the boys' lives but they act as metaphors for the different stages of their relationship. Andrew and Victor *are* the story, the essence of it:

> Wearing only a singlet and shorts, Victor looked unprotected, as if he had gone into battle without his armor. Possibly he felt unprotected too. Anyone who habitually went about wearing four or five layers of clothing was bound to feel at a loss when he took them off. If he was allowed to compete in his usual clothes, he might sweep the field, winning every event, if he weren't earthbound by the weight.

Here is Andrew, a very different kind of person, but also another loner:

> Then he found a lump on his neck and hoped that his tonsils might be swelling up, but he couldn't make them hurt, no matter how hard he prodded. He looked at his watch. It was a quarter to nine. He thought, in exactly twelve hours' time the bus will be stopping in Polthorpe and I shall be walking up the path into school. The very thought was enough to give him a clutching sort of pain, exactly where he thought his heart must be, but it passed away, almost before he had time to feel it. He went over to the window and looked out, kneeling on the floor with his chin wedged against the sill.

The difference between them is summed up by Victor's comment "I don't want to learn things; I'd rather just find out." Andrew, on the other hand, is much happier doing what he is told to do. This kind of writing is similar to that of Paula Fox, who, in *Portrait of Ivan* and *The Stone-Faced Boy*, moves the plotless novel almost to the point where the author is in danger of losing the reader: there is a welter of extraneous detail and events that are, seemingly, not germane. Paula Fox, however, does manage to reassure us that she knows what she is doing; by the end of the story we know the relevance of that attention to detail and why certain incidents that seemed so unimportant at the time were included. But there are moments in *Thunder and Lightnings* when Jan Mark seems to be flying dangerously by the seat of her pants, moments when she really is unsure which direction the book is taking — what follows is there only because there has to be something — anything — that happens next. The two opening pages of chapter thirteen are a good example. What is happening sounds flat and inconsequential; the prose, accordingly, becomes clumsy. The description of the wind being "like a mean child who jeered round corners and disappeared when you followed it" is a feeble grasping after effect compared with, say, the scene in chapter eleven where the boys are looking at an ordnance map "patterned all over with the ghostly bones of dead airfields."

Thunder and Lightnings, good though it may be, *is* a first novel, and close examination of the text reveals uncertainties and weaknesses — the strained, too literary image; the incident that has no real purpose — that disappear in its successors. *Under the Autumn Garden* may be a less appealing book, but it is more subtle. Matthew, the central character, does not possess Andrew's cool intelligence, nor does he have Victor's attractive energy; there is less humor and what remains of it is more sardonic, and the adults are either unsympathetic or rather nasty. But there are very few weak moments in the writing. A house is described as having a "roof like a quilt thrown over an unmade bed" and Matthew at one point says "She goes on, whaa-whaa-whaa, just like a chain saw." In this second apparently plotless novel, the author now seems to be in control of all the different elements. It isn't without story in quite the same way as *Thunder and Lightnings*. It consists of several small stories that illustrate the various areas of Matthew's life — the history project at school; the Bagnalls and their six cats;

the attempt to establish the fact that Sir Oliver of Hoxenham really existed; the unhappy relationship with the children of the builder who is repairing the house next door. In each of these a crisis occurs, and Matthew, being a rather weak character who lacks sufficient inner resources and strengths to face trouble, comes almost to the point of breakdown. (This is exactly the same theme as *Divide and Rule*, but in the latter work Jan Mark explores it more powerfully.) Matthew in fact does not break down, and the ending of the book, with the discovery of Sir Oliver's ring, suggests a note of cautious optimism, of recovery.

This is symbolized very effectively by the hole Matthew has been digging, which is the most striking image in the book. Trying to uncover the garden and search for the remains of a medieval priory is a ridiculous thing to do, quite beyond the abilities of one boy, and it is not surprising that nobody will take him very seriously. As the novel progresses, however, the function of the hole becomes more metaphorical than actual — it is Matthew burying his head in the sand, hiding away from unpleasant realities. Indeed, for one brief moment, it becomes a sort of troglodyte dwelling, used by the horrible Angel girls as a house. They, too, are running away from reality, but, unfortunately, they cannot understand Matthew's problems, nor he theirs. Eventually the hole ceases to have any point as symbol or actuality, and Matthew is forbidden to dig in it any longer. By this stage he no longer cares — he has stopped running away. He suffers from having no outlet for his anger. "That's a good fuel, anger," Victor says in *Thunder and Lightnings*. So it may be, up to a point: Victor cannot respond angrily to his mother's unfair treatment of him, but at least he can come third in a race when the rest of the school laugh at him for entering it. Matthew is in a worse situation. He is thwarted at every turn, and, without the ability to hit back, he allows his anger and frustration to turn in on himself where it operates, of course, destructively.

As with its predecessor, the texture of *Under the Autumn Garden* is extremely rich. The patterns of rural life are once again part of the story — we are in the same village, and some of the characters in *Thunder and Lightnings* play minor roles in this novel. There is the same verbal dexterity, the point made in a few striking words:

> Matthew reflected that people were not, after all, interested in his school work. They were only interested in him doing it.

And a similar use is made of detail that is seemingly irrelevant, but which provides an illuminating comment on character and situation:

> The sands and the sea were empty: he walked down to the edge of the water and sat there, letting the buzz go out of his ears. A little flat dog minced along the sand, glanced at Matthew, and sat down a few yards away, courteously looking out to sea instead of grinning at him after the fashion of solitary dogs. After a while it got up and walked quietly away. He was almost sorry to see it go.
>
> It was such a gentlemanly dog.

Matthew is courteous, gentlemanly, "flat" — too much so: these attributes almost ruin him. It is interesting that this passage is the only point in the book where the sea is mentioned, and yet Matthew lives only a short distance from the beach. This is right, for he cannot yet find himself in the vast expanses that sea and sand imply; his head and his heart are buried in a hole.

If there is a weakness in *Under the Autumn Garden*, it is that neither the reader nor Matthew discover until almost the end of the book that Mrs. Angel has left home and abandoned her children. It is true that the story demands that this information be hidden from the reader, but there is no convincing reason why Matthew's parents should not tell him. This is the only moment when it is difficult to believe in what is happening, so that the ultimate disclosure of the fact seems artificially contrived. No such weakness is apparent in Jan Mark's third novel, *The*

Ennead. At first sight, nothing more different from its predecessors could be imagined. Rural Norfolk has been replaced by life on Erato, a planet in a remote galaxy; we are in the future instead of the present; it is about adults, not children; it is science fiction rather than the expected children's novel, with a well-organized, fast-moving story-line, a plot instead of incidents, action instead of metaphor, image, and dense texture. But the themes of the book are a development of those explored in *Under the Autumn Garden.* Once again, *The Ennead* is a story about the struggle of the individual to remain alive, his integrity intact, in a wholly alien and hostile society. Here, in a novel which is much more likely to be read by teenagers than younger children, it is possible to go further; there is no hope at the end: Eleanor, Moshe, and Isaac opt for an almost certain death rather than submit to the stultifying prurient mores of Erato. How much should one compromise in order to find a place in the world is a question *The Ennead* poses: how far should one conform to a morality that entirely ruins the good in people? Not at all, Jan Mark seems to be saying. Isaac, who has posed as a conformist for the whole of his life, has had most of his natural fellow-feeling destroyed; but not quite all: in helping Eleanor to escape from the wrath of the inhabitants of Epsilon, he knows he will suffer the same fate as she will. The one area of unselfishness left in him is his undoing.

The message is bleak, but not totally despairing. Moshe, Isaac and Eleanor have courage and a tremendous inner toughness; Moshe and Eleanor have dignity as well, and an ability to love. On Erato, where population control, dislike, suspicion, and minding everybody else's business are the norm, such people are particularly vulnerable. Even inspecting a mural is seen as an anti-social act:

> "What are you doing, looking at our wall?" Barnet demanded.
>
> "Isn't it meant to be looked at?"

Human love — particularly sexual love — is frowned on more than anything else:

Isaac, like everyone else, cast about covertly for the said fornicator. Don't be seen not wondering. No name was ever mentioned on such occasions; the threat was enough. Whoever the message was for knew that it was for him.

One is reminded of the follies of extreme puritan theocracies such as that of the original settlers in New England and the witch-hunts that led to the tragedies in Salem; and indeed Eleanor is exposed and pursued almost as if she was a witch. Arthur Miller says in his preface to *The Crucible*: "Sex, sin, and the Devil were early linked, and so they continued to be in Salem, and are today . . . Our opposites are always robed in sexual sin."

But *The Ennead*, of course, is not a historical novel: it is about a future that has its seeds in our immediate present. It is a picture of what life may well be like in a world that becomes too obsessed with population control, a world in which we abdicate our responsibilities to ourselves and each other and hand our consciences over to some outside authority such as the Church or the State. This theme is also explored by Peter Dickinson in *The Blue Hawk* and, to a lesser extent, in *Tulku*, though both these novels are written by someone with a very different cast of mind. *The Ennead* is not a bleak novel in emphasizing the fact that without the capacity to love, to be unselfish, to have courage to continue to make our own moral decisions, we cease to be viable human beings, and that when Authority will not allow us to be viable human beings, we are better off dead.

Parts of *The Ennead* portray the struggle between the individual and the dictates of organized religion, and Jan Mark's fourth novel, *Divide and Rule*, is almost wholly concerned with this struggle. (The parallel with Peter Dickinson's *The Blue Hawk* is even stronger here.) We are, once more, in a strange alien world, remote in place and time, but precisely where and when we are not told. This doesn't matter; the vagueness helps to universalize the message: the points made can be applied to *any* theocratic society.

The story concerns Hanno, an eighteen-year-old boy, who is chosen by an absurd ritualistic mumbo-jumbo — so old that any meaning and purpose it may have had has long since been lost — to be the temple Shepherd for one year. (The idea is not unlike a similar ritual performed by a moribund society in *The Tombs of Atuan* by Ursula Le Guin.) This means he has to live inside the temple and have very little to occupy himself with; the Shepherd is never required to do anything. Hanno is utterly unfitted for this role. Cheerful, but not very bright, almost loutish, he is an unbeliever, interested only in the physical — the outdoor life and sleeping with girls. He cannot cope. Snubbed and left alone by the other officials, he begins to suffer a mental and emotional breakdown which becomes total when he finds that the temple rites, supposed to be unchanging ever since the beginning of civilization, are being altered for some rather sinister purposes — financial gain, and an attempt to increase the Church's control of the people by making new converts. At the end of the book, when his year is up, he is an outcast, almost blind, speechless, shunned by everybody.

His efforts to retain his integrity are concentrated in attempts to escape from his prison, and to expose the priest as a fraud. Not only does he fail every time — he hasn't the ability to outwit the authorities — but he always does the wrong thing, thus making his situation worse than it was. He is more sheep than shepherd, more body than brain. Indeed the author draws attention to this more than once by suggesting that his name is like the sound of a sheep bleating. The other famous Hanno in contemporary children's fiction is the gorilla in Lucy Boston's *A Stranger at Green Knowe*, and maybe a parallel is intended. Both Hannos are unfortunate victims of an alien environment; neither can cope, and Jan Mark's Hanno is, physically, a bit of a gorilla — a big, shambling youth of little intelligence.

The message is similar to that of *The Ennead*. State or Church will go to any lengths to make the individual conform, and those that can't or won't conform are eliminated.

It is a more disturbing book than *The Ennead*, because Hanno, likeable though he is, lacks the qualities we see in Moshe and Eleanor. The scheming, plotting Isaac — a typical example of the reed who bends in the wind — would have had a very successful and enjoyable year in the temple, but Hanno cannot bend. One major difference from *The Ennead* — and this makes *Divide and Rule* a novel of even less hope than its predecessor — is that the author seems to be implying here that if we want to survive we must force ourselves, for a time, into a pretense of conforming. Individual and society in *Divide and Rule* are totally at loggerheads. Which brings us back to *Thunder and Lightnings* and Andrew's mother:

> There's no such thing as fairness. It's a word made up to keep children quiet. When you discover it's a fraud, then you're starting to grow up.

Adulthood, Jan Mark seems to be saying in all her books, is at best messy, at worst brutish and nasty; the growing up processes involve coming to terms with these facts and making of them what you will — but if you totally reject the demands of authority, however worthy and fine your motives may be, you won't be able to escape punishment.

Aquarius, Jan Mark's most recent novel, is as harsh and bleak as its predecessors. Once again we are in an unnamed country at an unspecified date, though the technology of the inhabitants suggests a time no later than the early Middle Ages. The central character, Viner, gets his name from his craft — that of a water diviner — but he finds he is living in the wrong place; his village is subjected to constant rain and almost nonstop flooding. The local people think he actually causes the rain, and drive him away. On his travels he reaches a country where there is unprecedented drought; the wells are drying up, and all the efforts of Morning Light, the rain-maker and king, to produce water are useless. Viner, after finding several new wells, becomes popular and politically powerful, but he refuses an arranged marriage that would make him the monarch: he is sexually attracted to Morning Light, and guesses, rightly,

that the rain-king's gifts are the opposite of what is supposed — he causes droughts. He abducts Morning Light
(considerable physical violence is involved in this) and takes
him back to his own village: Viner has now got what he
wants — status among his *own* people, and the man he
desires is his virtual prisoner:

> . . . the water was tamed, the village was secure, the
> people content, and Viner their saviour. He smiled be-
> nignly upon them, and upon Morning Light, inspired
> at last, dancing in despair beneath the blue sky, the
> fleeting clouds, the inexorable sun.

This is not a book for the backward reader. The prose
makes few compromises — adult vocabulary often densely
packed with imagery, long complex sentences — but almost always it is an effective instrument:

> The bridge was thriftily built at the river's narrowest
> point within the village boundary, and that circum-
> stance, coupled with the fact that the two piles which
> supported the centre span forced the water into tur-
> bulent rapids, ensured that the bridge was under con-
> stant assault from the pressure of the torrent beneath
> it, the author of its own destruction.

We have come a long way from the apparent simplicity of
Thunder and Lightnings.

Aquarius has a well-constructed absorbing narrative, full
of memorable characters and exciting incident — one
thinks in particular of the scenes in which people struggle
for political power when the rain-king is known to be a
broken man — and it has many fine descriptive passages
dealing with landscape and weather. The landscape is entirely fictitious, but it is made very real: "Nightfall found
him limping among rubble on a blasted hillside where
nothing stood except the dead bracken that crisped and
crinkled underfoot" — and there is from time to time a
skillful use of simile that is terse and evocative: "holding
his breath and trembling like the dry twigs all about him."

There is no happy future ahead, at the end of the book,
for Viner's relationship with Morning Light. Morning Light

now hates Viner more than any other living person. The message is that in struggling for status people manipulate and use one another to the extent that love can be totally destroyed; that those who get exactly what they want may do immense harm to others and lose their own humanity. Affection, Jan Mark is saying, contains the seeds of possessiveness, and possessiveness is the opposite of freedom, for both parties concerned.

Scarcely anyone writing today presents youth with a more somber picture of life than does Jan Mark. Sometimes the reader may feel that her novels go to an extreme beyond which it is not possible to venture in books for children and teenagers. This doesn't matter: the harsh truths of her vision of the world are infinitely preferable to the cozy pap that is sometimes served up for the young.

References

JAN MARK
> *Thunder and Lightnings* Kestrel 1976; Crowell 1979
> *Under the Autumn Garden* Kestrel 1977; Crowell 1979
> *The Ennead* Kestrel 1978; Crowell 1978
> *Divide and Rule* Kestrel 1979; Crowell 1980
> *Aquarius* Kestrel 1982

LUCY BOSTON
> *A Stranger at Green Knowe* Faber 1961; Harcourt 1961

PETER DICKINSON
> *The Blue Hawk* Gollancz 1976; Atlantic/Little, Brown 1976
> *Tulku* Gollancz; Dutton 1979

PAULA FOX
> *Portrait of Ivan* Bradbury 1969; Macmillan, London, 1969
> *The Stone-Faced Boy* Bradbury 1968; Macmillan, London, 1968

PETER HUNT
> "Whatever Happened to Jan Mark?" in *Signal 31*, January 1980

URSULA LE GUIN
> *The Tombs of Atuan* Atheneum 1971; Gollancz 1971

ARTHUR MILLER
> *The Crucible* Viking 1953; Cresset 1956

ROBERT WESTALL
The Machine-Gunners Macmillan, London, 1975; Greenwillow 1976
"How Real Do You Want Your Realism?" in *Signal 28*, January 1979

Real and Transcendental

JANE LANGTON

Americans sometimes say — perhaps forgetting Ursula Le Guin — that fantasy in children's books is a peculiarly British product. It is probably indisputable that the British have written more fantasy than the Americans, and more of a higher quality: the work of Philippa Pearce, Alan Garner, and Penelope Lively, for example, is not matched by many American authors. It may well be because the British writer so often lives surrounded by the visible signs of history, and fantasy increasingly is a way in which the British children's author brings the past alive. Penelope Lively's *The Wild Hunt of the Ghost Hounds* was inspired by her living near Exmoor with its ancient legends of the ghostly hunt; Alan Garner's *Red Shift* by the Roman and seventeenth-century relics near his home in Cheshire. Indeed, the traditional historical novel, if not dead, is decidedly out of fashion, positively discouraged by publishers. "Children don't read that sort of thing any more," is a frequent cry. It isn't that America has no history, but that in many parts of the United States the past is less obvious or sometimes too recent for people to think it worthy of resurrection in a children's story.

One American author well-known as a writer of fantasy springing from history is Jane Langton. (Well-known at least in the United States; none of her books is currently in print in England, which is a great pity — her writing has an appeal that is much more than the merely local.) She lives in Massachusetts, a state of the Union with a past longer and more evident than most; her books are nearly all set there, and in her fantasies she often explores various facets of local history. She returns in her novels again and again to

Concord, famous for its associations with Louisa May Alcott and with the Transcendentalists, Thoreau and Emerson; it was also an early Puritan settlement and, in 1775,
"from behind each fence and farm-yard wall," the scene of
the first shots to be fired in the War of Independence. Here,
obviously, is a place with a great deal of interesting, visible
history, and, like many British authors in similar surroundings, she has elected to write about that past, not in the
medium of the standard historical novel, but through fantasy. Her feeling for the past is well summed up in this
passage from *The Astonishing Stereoscope*:

> Looking at the familiar houses Eleanor thought again,
> as she did so often, that they were sitting on their own
> past. Here in Concord, Massachusetts, it was hard to
> forget that *now* was not only *now* but also *then*. She
> was putting her feet down, *tramp, tramp*, in the foot-
> steps of Ralph Waldo Emerson, or Henry Thoreau, or
> Louisa May Alcott, or some minuteman who had fired
> a shot at the North Bridge. And even when she
> breathed the air she couldn't help remembering what
> Uncle Freddy always said about it, that it was the air
> of freedom. On this October day the air of Concord
> was cool and brisk, smelling slightly of skunk.

Yet it is sometimes forgotten that Jane Langton is also a
creator of realistic stories. Three of her seven novels for
children contain no element of the fantastic, except for
what goes on inside the head of the central character of *The
Majesty of Grace* and *The Boyhood of Grace Jones*; but that
is fantasy in a different sense of the word. These books
show a marked contrast to the mass of the most recent
American realistic children's fiction. They have a distinctly
old-fashioned air about them, and they are none the worse
for that. Jane Langton's novels have a strong sense of being
the products of a New England influence; the writing, the
material, the view of life, the moral values, the children at
the center of the stories give the reader the feeling that the

author is aware of, and in tune with, a particular and special place. This cannot be said about every writer; S. E. Hinton's books, for example, are obviously set in a city in the United States, but where? It doesn't seem to matter.

The Majesty of Grace is Jane Langton's first novel. Its main theme is original and entertaining; Grace Jones thinks she is the long-lost elder sister of the princesses Elizabeth and Margaret (the events take place in the nineteen thirties) and that one day she will be the Queen of England. Some of the best writing in the book revolves around this idea:

> Grace tried to throw herself off the bike, but it was going so fast that now she couldn't lose her balance even though she wanted to. She gave herself up for lost. But even in her last moments she found time to imagine a wistful scene. She, Grace, was lying in a velvet-lined coffin in Westminster Abbey while the whole population of the British Isles filed reverently by, gazing with sorrow at the beautiful young princess who was never to take her rightful place upon the throne.

Unfortunately, this central theme is lost in a welter of other events — the problems with the neighbors, Dad losing his job because of the Depression, and so on; the result is that the structure of the book is a bit too loose. However, these secondary ideas are always interesting and well-handled, often with an engaging sense of humor. The scene in which Sophie, Grace's younger sister, tries to talk on the telephone with her father's ex-boss, Mr. Post, is delightful comedy; a little overdone maybe, but very funny nevertheless. It doesn't advance the narrative — indeed it's a complete episode in itself; but it's so well-done that the loss of the story line here does not seem to matter.

The ending of the book is somewhat contrived. Pop gets his job back; the family acquire a new car; all their treasured possessions are taken out of pawn; Will makes his radio set work; Grace finds the missing piece of the jigsaw

puzzle: it's all too much of an unreal happily-ever-after conclusion. However, *The Majesty of Grace* is a first novel by
a writer of considerable talent; its weaknesses come from a
lack of experience rather than poor invention or dull characterization. Particularly memorable is Jane Langton's ren-
dering of sounds: the telephone, "Brrinngg!;" car horns, "Ah-
-OOGA, Ah-OOGA!;" a record of Sir Harry Lauder singing
"Roamin' in the Gloamin'" on a wind-up gramophone that
hasn't been sufficiently wound up, "my-Y-y-Y-y-Y-y La-a-A-
a-A-a-SSIE-ie-IE-ie-IE-ie." Few writers even attempt such onomatopoeia, let alone bring it off successfully.

In *The Boyhood of Grace Jones* the central character is
now starting junior high school, but she is just as wrapped
up in a fantasy world as she was in the previous book. The
preoccupations of her friends, Dot and Teenie Moon, with
boys, fashion, and make-up, seem quite contemptible to
her; much more important are the heroes and heroines of
her reading — "Tom of *The Flying Cloud,* Trueblue Tom,
that swashbuckling daring young sailor," and Captain
Nancy Blackett of Arthur Ransome's *Swallows and Amazons.* Grace wishes she was a boy; she dresses like one,
cuts her hair short, and cares absolutely nothing about what
other people think of her. "What an odd child!" — her
teacher says — "why doesn't she behave like a normal girl?
There must be something basically, psychologically wrong
with her, deep down inside." Yet by the end of the story
this archetypal tomboy has been transformed into a "real"
girl, in love with her music teacher and experimenting with
Dot Moon's lipsticks. The idea is not particularly original,
and the resolution of the story seems to suggest unfortunately that the stereotypical norm — what girls are *supposed* to be — is more to be desired than exploring the
consequences of being unconventional. *The Boyhood of
Grace Jones,* I imagine, would make a militant feminist
seethe with rage, and I don't myself feel comfortable with
Grace's conversion to "Whispering and giggling in high spirits, and comparing the pictures of movie stars on the lids
of their Dixie cups," even though it is perhaps right for the

period of the book. An opposite view of this is put forward in Gene Kemp's *The Turbulent Term of Tyke Tiler*: a contemporary story in which the boyishness of the heroine is something to be rejoiced in. Gene Kemp's novel won the Carnegie Medal in 1977, which suggests that the children's book establishment is at last taking note of what feminists have long been preaching: that belief in some male and female "norm" of manners, behavior, and family role is in part responsible for the inferior position of women in society.

That said, there are many pleasures en route in *The Boyhood of Grace Jones*. Characterization is excellent — a crowd of well-observed kids, with hard-faced Teenie being particularly convincing — and there is a great deal of entertaining incident and witty dialogue. The writing constantly sparkles with good humor and original, unusual language:

> "The flutes here at the beginning are just a pretty little babbling brook," said Mr. Chester, leaning over the twin girls who were the orchestra's flute section, Dolores and Dorothy Murphy, his less-than-an-eighth-of-an-inch of fat less than eight inches away from their twin faces. " Tiddily-tiddily, tiddily-tiddily, tiddily-tiddily-tiddle. Do you see, flutes?"
>
> Nearly fainting with rapture, the Murphy twins lifted their flutes and blew into them. "Whiff-puffety-whiff," they huffed, their lips pursed, their eyes crossed because Mr. Chester was standing so close. "Whiff-whiffety-whiff."

Grace's enthusiastic discovery of poetry is also seen as both admirable and amusing. She washes up dishes chanting *The Ancient Mariner*, and at the end of the book when she's written some of her own, she's bold enough to cry, "Move over, Samuel Taylor Coleridge!" The ambitions and limitations of the young adolescent are, in this novel, extremely well expressed.

Paper Chains is the most recent of Jane Langton's realistic stories, and I think the most successful. It is her only book that belongs to the young adult category; it portrays the life of eighteen-year-old Evelyn Underhill in her first semester at college — a similar theme to Rodie Sudbery's *Ducks and Drakes*, a less successful novel. The plot derives from a well-worn theme of second-rate romantic fiction: the plain, ordinary heroine — she's too tall and her teeth are as big as tombstones — falls in love with her classics professor who remains quite unaware of her infatuation, but nice young George, who appears first as a pretzel seller but is in fact a fellow student, wins her heart in the end. It sounds ordinary, but the remarkable thing about *Paper Chains* is how well Jane Langton handles such conventional material. Her achievement lies in the characterization of Evelyn and her friends, the realistic details of the start of university life — room-sharing, parties, work assignments, nights out at the movies — and, above all, the sense of humor, sometimes ironic, sometimes farcical, that is present on nearly every page. Kayo, Evelyn's roommate, arty, eccentric, and ultimately a drop-out; Frankie, naïve but attractive, who can't say no to the boys; "pompous prudish putrid Prue;" Archie, the Marxist, constantly in trouble because of his dog rather than his political opinions; Red Fred, lunatic and irresponsible; Evelyn herself, always undervaluing her own worth as a person and as an academic: they make a fine gallery of rounded portraits of real people.

The zany humor of much of the book is well illustrated by the six "unsendable letters" Evelyn writes to her classics professor; they are indeed never mailed to him, but are useful as an outlet, helping her get her feelings under control:

> *Maybe you are Jesus Christ come back to earth as a humble professor of classics! And nobody knows but me! Except of course for Lady Godiva, that other girl who sits in the front row, the one with the long golden hair pouring over her shoulders, back, front, knees, feet and toes. (No, no, forget Lady Godiva. I'm sorry I brought her up.)*
>
> *I noticed in class today that you were wearing a dirty shirt. I hope this is a clue to the mysterious life*

you lead outside of class. I think it must mean you are a bachelor.

The only fault in this novel is the paper chains of the title — Christmas decorations — which are a symbol of the unknown years stretching ahead as well as the years of growth Evelyn has left behind. In the last chapter, attention is drawn rather clumsily to their symbolic function: it is as if the author didn't quite know how to end the book, and felt, wrongly, that the beginning of Evelyn's relationship with George was not a significant enough way to bring matters to a conclusion. The last three pages sound as if they belong to a story in another genre. However, it is a small fault. It is refreshing to read a young adult novel in which problems do not loom large on every page, in which the reader is allowed for once to take pleasure in the mental and emotional development of the central character.

The fantasies, *The Diamond in the Window, The Swing in the Summerhouse, The Astonishing Stereoscope,* and *The Fledgling* are all concerned with the adventures of the same family — Eddy and Eleanor Hall; Georgie Dorian who becomes their cousin when Uncle Fred Hall marries her mother, Alex. Rather dotty Aunt Alex and Uncle Fred try to earn a living by turning their bizarre Victorian house into a school, the Concord College of Transcendentalist Knowledge. The characterization is as sharp, the humor as amusing, as in the other novels, and although the use of ideas and language borrowed from Emerson and Thoreau is subtle, it is never at a level that stretches beyond the grasp of the child reader. Fred Hall, in fact, is a parody of Emerson and Thoreau, and, mainly through him, the author's attitudes — complex and contradictory — to the Transcendentalists are revealed. Much about them she admires: their feelings for nature; their views, influenced by Wordsworth and Rousseau, of childhood; their unquenchable optimism. But they, she implies, like Uncle Fred, were often ridiculous and impractical, and their use of language could be inept or derivative. Some of Fred's ultra-enthusiastic pronouncements are an effective parody of the language, the bounding optimism, and the failure, at times, of the Transcendentalists to make real communication with ordinary people. When Eleanor asks him, in *The Astonishing Stereoscope*, what is the Unforgivable Sin, does Hell exist, and why are there so many different religions, his answer is so far above her comprehension that her mind wanders; she examines her face in the mirror to see if her looks are improving:

> "The religious impulse," he cried, striding back and forth. "One, the basic, primitive, mystic sense of awe. Two! The worship of a martyred hero. Three! The eternal that makes for righteousness. Four! The divine in nature. Five! The divine in man. Has the primordial religious impulse awakened in you at last, my pet?"
>
> "Well," said Eleanor doubtfully, "I don't . . ."
>
> But Uncle Freddy didn't stop to listen. He went right on. And on and on and on. Eleanor discovered that she could just see herself in the mirror over the mantelpiece behind the parlor table.

In *The Swing in the Summerhouse* she quite rightly gets annoyed with her uncle's lack of worldly talents. His inability to make any money she sees as leading her and Eddy not to missing the basic necessities of life but to being deprived of some of its pleasures. Jane Langton is here thinking of the impracticality of the Transcendentalist utopia, maybe in particular of the selfish philosopher, Bronson Alcott. In *The Diamond in the Window*, when Fred tries to throw the bathers out of Walden Pond and is arrested by the police — an amusing and at the same time rather sad episode — the Transcendentalists' genuine creativity is shown as coming close to becoming mere eccentricity.

The fantasy sections of the first three of these books are a weakness: Each section is a self-contained scene, not part of a chapter with a continuous narrative, and this leaves the whole story with a disjointed feeling; throughout *The Diamond in the Window* and in parts of *The Swing in the Summerhouse* these scenes don't make much comment on or have direct relevance to the realistic tale of the Hall family's everyday life that is running parallel to the fantasy. In *The Diamond in the Window*, in particular, the language is inadequate in suggesting the full experience the children undergo:

> Prince Krishna's face was flaming. He dropped his book, and they both bent to pick it up, bumping their heads together. Aunt Lily stood up, laughing. But Prince Krishna's face when he stood up had an expression so serious and loving that she stopped laughing and bent her head. He took her hand, with a beautiful gentle gesture, and spoke to her softly. Aunt Lily looked down at the snow, then gave him her other hand. Then she looked up at him and smiled, and turned quickly and hurried away. Her long skirts passed near Eleanor, and looking up at her, Eleanor could see that her face glowed with happiness. Prince Krishna just stood where he was, his face, too, radiant with love, as he watched her go.

There are too many vague adjectives; nothing is observed with precision. "Expression so serious and loving," "a beautiful gentle gesture," "glowed with happiness," "radiant with love" are the threadbare clichés of romantic magazines. Linguistically, *The Diamond in the Window* is the least satisfactory of all Jane Langton's books; the adult reader becomes bored quite early on in what is, by the usual standards of children's fiction, a rather long novel.

The Swing in the Summerhouse, though still very episodic, is an improvement. The introduction of Georgie, the girl next door, as a major character, is an excellent idea; her amusing eccentricities make a neat contrast to down-to-earth Eddy and emotional Eleanor. Some, though not all, of the fantasy scenes comment directly on the realistic action. The chapter "What Are You Worth?" provides Eleanor with some of the answers to her questions about the family's financial problems; not everything, she discovers, can be measured in terms of money. In the fantasy sequence she unwittingly sells her baby cousin for 876,542 dollars, and can only get him back by returning all the cash to the bank till:

> The machine wanted more. Five hundred thousand dollars wasn't enough. What a nasty bargain this was turning out to be! Eleanor felt soiled and grubby. She reached a trembling hand into her skirt once more and counted out another hundred thousand dollars. "Here's some more," she said, her voice quavering. "All this is for you." Then she transferred her skirt to her wounded right hand so that she could hit the CASH button with her left. Bang! "Oh, oh!" Eleanor flapped her hand up and down to see if the drawer was opening. It wasn't.

"Soiled and grubby" and that terse "it wasn't" are a much more individual use of English than "a beautiful gentle gesture."

The action in *The Astonishing Stereoscope* hinges on one crucial scene early in the book. John Green, a pupil of Uncle Fred's, climbs on to the roof of the house to hammer in a support for a loudspeaker — it's part of a Hallowe'en trick. He falls off and is taken to the hospital, where he remains in a coma for almost the rest of the story. When he falls he is trying to help Eddy, who has disobediently joined him on the ridge of the attic gable; at the same moment, Eleanor, indoors, is pretending to be a witch and chanting, "I have put a curse on this house! I have made a pact with the Devil himself! A curse! A curse! A curse upon this house!" *Both* children, therefore, feel responsible for the accident, and, until John Green regains consciousness, they experience an appalling sense of guilt which they attempt to expiate by turning to religion, Eleanor wholeheartedly and Eddy somewhat reluctantly. Not many contemporary children's writers attempt to portray a child's religious experiences (Peter Dickinson is an interesting exception.) *The Astonishing Stereoscope* is not only unusual in doing so, but Jane Langton views even this with her customary ironic humor. Eddy and Eleanor sample the different brands on offer in Concord — the Roman Catholic Church, the First

Parish Church — and in the fantasy episodes (again, unfortunately, only some of them are properly linked to the main theme) they visit a medieval cathedral, a human sacrifice at Stonehenge, and the Puritan chapel in seventeenth-century Concord. The children don't make any choices; in fact they find something repellent about every single one of these experiences. "How can you drink blood? That's just terrible," Eleanor says to the bewildered young Catholic priest; and the Puritans' catechism class they find insufferably boring. Miss Brisket, the gushing and hopelessly inefficient Sunday School teacher at the First Parish Church, is one of the book's delights, though one can scarcely believe the author's note that "Miss Brisket is myself." It's a very accurate observation of the wrong person doing the wrong job:

> "Arthur Downs," cried the teacher, "you sit down right here next to Cecily. George Pitman, you just get right off of Jimmy and sit over here beside me. Well, what's this we have here? A new student? Why, what a nice surprise. What is your name, dear? My, isn't that a pretty name! Isn't that a pretty dress! Now, class, first we'll have the lesson, and then we'll do our project for the day." Miss Brisket rushed to the blackboard, snatched up a piece of chalk, stared horrorstruck at a huge drawing of a monster eating a horse, erased it swiftly, and began writing the lesson.

None of this makes the reader uncomfortable; religion itself isn't mocked, nor is a child's interest in why there are so many versions of Christianity being laughed at. "God," Uncle Freddy tells Eleanor, "is truth and righteousness and justice and beauty and love and joy." There is nothing ironic in that statement.

The Fledgling, however, is the most satisfying of these four books, because fantasy and realism are firmly woven together, and the language has at times a poetry, austere and controlled, that is missing from the other three. It's fall; the wild geese are flying south, and an old goose lets

Georgie ride on his back, then teaches her how to fly. (Penelope Farmer's first novel, *The Summer Birds,* is concerned with a similar theme, but it is not as well written as *The Fledgling.*)

> She was filled with delight. The wind blew her hair streaming away from her face, it rippled the hems of her pajamas, and it breathed cool on her bare feet as she lay like a feather between the churning wings, looking down at the houses rushing away below her.

It is as if Jane Langton's linguistic ability were transformed from the serviceable and adequate into the perfect instrument for her purposes. There is in *The Fledgling* a use of rhythm and cadence, a care over choice of words and an attention to sound as well as meaning, that is absent from the previous novels:

> And nothing woke her until morning, not even the racket in the sky just after she fell asleep, as a last tardy flock of wild geese flew over the house, cleaving the air in a battering plunge, heading for Walden Pond, eager to break the fragile ice with the fury of their clamorous descent. Low over the peaked roof and domed tower of Georgie's house they were shouting at each other, *Go DOWN! go DOWN! follow ME! follow WHERE? right THERE? over THERE? no, HERE! come HERE! come HERE! HERE! HERE! right HERE! come DOWN! right HERE!*

Mr. Preek's metamorphosis from a bumbling nuisance into a real villain may not be psychologically convincing, but Miss Prawn's development from an irritating busybody into an almost insane old woman does seem right. Planting her front garden with plastic roses that spell out the words "Welcome to Concord" is not only excruciatingly bad taste, but the opposite of all that is finest in Thoreau and Emerson; the reader is delighted when Georgie towards the end of the book removes most of these monstrosities. Mr. Preek and Miss Prawn are an effective contrast to Georgie and the goose: evil is pitted against good, and, as in real life, it nearly prevails. The goose is shot dead. Evil, as personified in Mr. Preek, cannot take pleasure in the mysterious, the beautiful, the unquantifiable elements in the universe — here a girl flying on a goose's back — and, because he is frightened by what he cannot understand, he has to destroy it to restore sense and propriety to his own narrow selfish existence. Georgie survives to mourn, but also to rejoice, because the goose has left her a present, a ball that in the dark becomes a magical globe showing the whole world:

> The blue surface of the ball was streaked with clouds, and below the clouds Georgie could catch glimpses of great land masses, of dark continents and snow-covered ice caps and deep jungles and blue oceans and lofty mountain ranges — the Andes, the Alps, the Himalayas.
>
> "Oh," breathed Georgie. "It's the world. It's the whole world."

The Fledgling is an achievement of a high order. The material, realistic and fantastic, is absolutely in balance and the prose is poetic, sensitive, and original; Jane Langton has here gone well beyond the limits of local history and Transcendentalist references. It has taken her a long time to knit together satisfactorily the various elements of her fantasies. Should she write another story about the Hall family, or a fantasy of a quite different nature, one would expect a fine book: she's arrived at a creative maturity.

References

JANE LANGTON
The Majesty of Grace Harper 1961
The Diamond in the Window Harper 1962; Hamish Hamilton 1969
The Swing in the Summerhouse Harper 1967; Hamish Hamilton 1970
The Astonishing Stereoscope Harper 1971
The Boyhood of Grace Jones Harper 1972
Paper Chains Harper 1977
The Fledgling Harper 1980

PENELOPE FARMER
  The Summer Birds Chatto 1962; Harcourt 1962
ALAN GARNER
  Red Shift Collins 1972; Macmillan, New York, 1973
GENE KEMP
  The Turbulent Term of Tyke Tiler Faber 1977; Merrimack 1980
PENELOPE LIVELY
  The Wild Hunt of Hagworthy Heinemann 1971; in America, as *The Wild Hunt of the Ghost Hounds* Dutton 1972
ARTHUR RANSOME
  Swallows and Amazons Cape 1930; Lippincott 1931
RODIE SUDBERY
  Ducks and Drakes Deutsch 1975

Medals and Awards

KATHERINE PATERSON

Few children's novelists have been given so many awards as Katherine Paterson. Four of her seven books have won major honors — the Newbery Medal for *Bridge to Terabithia* and *Jacob Have I Loved*, the National Book Award for *The Great Gilly Hopkins* and *The Master Puppeteer*; *The Great Gilly Hopkins* was also a Newbery Honor Book. This tells us something about the nature of her work and about the qualities that are looked for in children's fiction by those who give these awards. The National Book Award, the Newbery Medal, and the British equivalent of the latter, the Carnegie Medal, are what one might call the gifts of the children's literature "establishment;" the recipients on the whole — and there are certainly a few interesting and surprising exceptions — tend to write books that are conservative, fairly middle class, ("safe," in the sense of not questioning widely accepted values, might be a criticism) and above all, of high literary excellence. Let me say at once that I see nothing wrong with the criterion of high literary excellence. A novel for children should be judged, first and foremost, like any other novel — what merits does it have as a novel? How does it work as a piece of literature? Not: it is good because it has black kids in it, or because it deals with urban violence, or some aspect of life not dealt with elsewhere; no special pleading. It would be unlikely that Katherine Paterson, were she British, would receive The Other Award, for the kind of story she writes would not be of concern to the donors of that prize, the Children's Rights Workshop, who are particularly interested in books with an anti-sexist bias. There is nothing wrong with an institution like The Other Award; its intentions and the books it has honored are admirable, but it would be a sad day if the major establishment prizes were not given for works of high literary excellence.

Two Newbery Medals and two National Book Awards might imply that Katherine Paterson is the greatest living American writer of children's fiction; the purpose of this essay is not to assess whether she is or is not, but she certainly passes the test of literary excellence in all her books, particularly *Jacob Have I Loved*, which, using what one supposes are the criteria of the Newbery Medal Committee must be the most "deserving" novel in a long time. In fact, *Jacob Have I Loved* is such an advance on anything she had previously written — in background detail, imagery, characterization, above all in the sureness of tone of voice and sheer writing ability — that it casts doubts on whether her other award-winning books should have been singled out. Or maybe 1977 was not a good year? One of the unfortunate aspects of an annual prize is that one year may have half a dozen novels that deserve the Newbery or the Carnegie, but on another occasion the winner may be the best of an indifferent bunch. Also, those who give these honors are sometimes accused — rightly, on occasion — of picking the wrong book. The award, for instance, of the Carnegie Medal in 1969 to K. M. Peyton for the *Flambards* trilogy came in for considerable gunfire. And after comparing *Jacob Have I Loved* with *Bridge to Terabithia* the reader begins to think 1977 probably was not a good year.

One of the pleasures of reading Katherine Paterson's work is to notice the advance and development from *The Sign of the Chrysanthemum* and *Of Nightingales That Weep* to the kind of novel she is writing now. These early books are competent enough, but they give little indication of the excellence to come. A child may well be put off when he sees that their setting is medieval Japan, and finds on the first few pages of *Of Nightingales That Weep* lengthy acknowledgments, a historical note, and a glossary on the pronunciation of Japanese names. *The Sign of the Chrysanthemum* is the more approachable of the two; it is brief, tells an exciting story, and does not, as happens in *Of Nightingales That Weep*, take us on a detailed excursion into Japanese history — the complex warring feuds of the rival clans, the Heike and the Genji, that surrounded the Emperor. There are few signs here of the strongly individual characterization that marks Katherine Paterson's later books. Takanobu, the disgraced Samurai in *The Sign of the Chrysanthemum*, is a blustering, Falstaffian rogue who comes fully to life, but the other people, particularly the central characters in both novels, are two-dimensional figures. The task the author has set herself is, of course, immense — perhaps impossible: how can we know what it is like to be a child in twelfth-century Japan?

Both Muna in *The Sign of the Chrysanthemum* and Takiko in *Of Nightingales That Weep* have only one parent: Muna is illegitimate and spends much of the story looking for his father; Takiko's father is killed in battle in the opening chapter, and her relationship with her mother's second husband is far from satisfactory. Unhappy parent-child relationships are at the center of every one of Katherine Paterson's novels; the child who is — or who thinks he or she is — starved of love is an almost obsessional preoccupation of hers, the very wellspring, one would think, of her need to write:

> Something had happened to her mother in these weeks. Perhaps the potter was a devil and had bewitched her. Her soft, weeping mother had disappeared, and someone strong and cold had taken over her mother's beautiful body . . . Everything in her rejected the word *father*, for she was unable to consider that the monster was indeed her mother's husband and her own stepfather. (*Of Nightingales That Weep*)

"Rejected" is a key word in Katherine Paterson's work. The handling of this theme, and the considerable skill she shows in writing narrative — one turns the page, eager to find out what happens next — are the two main qualities that emerge in these first two books.

In *The Master Puppeteer* the writing has become more flexible and there are no chunks of ancient history that come between the story and the reader. We are still in Japan, in the eighteenth century this time; the violence and poverty of city life in that period, the deeds of Saburo the bandit (a sort of Oriental Robin Hood) and the efforts of the Shogun to capture him, give an exciting and colorful atmosphere to the narrative. The central character is a boy, Jiro, who leaves home to find employment in a local puppet theater, thus displeasing his father, who had hoped Jiro would learn his own trade, that of making puppets, and his mother, who regards his departure as very selfish. One reason Jiro leaves is that his poverty-stricken parents will now have one less mouth to feed, but his mother thinks he is shying away from his duty to contribute to the family income. Much of the book is taken up with Jiro's life at the theater — the friendships he forms with the other apprentices and his relationship with Yoshida, the director, who is bad-tempered and frightening, but at the same time almost a genius, utterly dedicated to his work.

When Jiro finds evidence that Saburo must be one of the theater's employees — he thinks at first, wrongly, that it is Yoshida himself — the political events are neatly entwined with the story and change from being merely a colorful backcloth into the main action. The master puppeteer is not only, therefore, a man who manipulates theatrical puppets, but a symbol for Saburo himself, a man who manipulates people. When Jiro discovers Saburo's real identity — the blind dramatist and chief reciter, Okada — the symbol has gathered another layer of meaning: Okada is more than a manipulator of people; he writes (as does the author herself, of course) the plots of their lives, too. Or at least he would like to. Jiro is in great danger, but Okada is foiled:

> "What does the master do when he catches a mouse with its jaws sunk deep into —"

> Jiro did not wait. He snatched the chest nearest him and threw it down between himself and the chanter.

He grabbed another and piled it on top. Then scrambling upon them to the rafters, he swung himself up like a monkey and slid across above Okada's head. When he was past him, he jumped from the rafter and pushed more boxes and chests into the passageway. The blind man had dropped the sword to the floor and was flailing his arms around helplessly, trying to find a way out of the trap that Jiro was throwing up around him.

But Okada, as I said, is a Robin Hood, not the Sheriff of Nottingham, and Jiro is certainly not on the side of the Shogun and the police. As in real life, it isn't easy to identify individuals in this book as wholly good or bad, and the way Okada and Jiro are reconciled to work together forms a subtle and satisfying conclusion to events. *The Master Puppeteer* has a very skillful narrative: probably the best in any of Katherine Paterson's novels.

Bridge to Terabithia is the author's first portrayal of the everyday world of children in modern America. It's the story of Jesse Owens, a misfit as the only boy in his family, with two older and two younger sisters. This is virtually the same situation as that of Ben Blewitt in *A Dog So Small* by Philippa Pearce — Ben suffers because he has two older siblings who are close friends, and two younger ones who are also more or less inseparable. But whereas the Blewitt parents are kindly disposed, if not very understanding, Jesse sees little of his father because of his work, and his mother has very little time for him apart from needing his help with the household chores. She shows him almost no affection. Though he is a tougher kid than Ben Blewitt, he, too, retreats from the real world: he becomes friendly with a girl, Leslie, who is also rather a misfit, and together they imagine a remote corner of the woods nearby is a kingdom, Terabithia, in which they are rulers. Leslie seeks Jesse out because she's an only child; her parents are both writers and retreat into *their* private worlds, and she is considered by the other kids at school to be strange and unsociable. The relationship between Leslie and Jesse is intense: it would not be wrong to think of them in a child-like way as lovers. Jesse's life comes crashing down in ruins when Leslie is accidentally drowned. Some of the finest writing in the book concerns his reactions and ultimate coming to terms with this sudden death:

> *Cremated.* Something clicked inside Jesse's head. That meant Leslie was gone. Turned to ashes. He would never see her again. Not even dead. Never. How could they dare? Leslie belonged to him. More to him than anyone in the world. No one had even asked him. No one had even told him. And now he was never going to see her again, and all they could do was cry. Not for Leslie. They weren't crying for Leslie. They were crying for themselves. Just themselves.

The ideas and their treatment in this part of the book are similar to those of *A Taste of Blackberries* by Doris Buchanan Smith, also a story of a child having to face up to the death of a close friend. Katherine Paterson's version is just as convincing and her writing skills are superior.

But *Bridge to Terabithia* has a number of faults. Jesse and many of the minor characters, particularly his teacher, Mrs. Myers, are strong, realistic creations, but Leslie is not altogether credible — too good to be true, mature beyond her years, almost faultless. It's a pity that she is observed only from the outside; we are never allowed to see into her head. Also, the Terabithia sections of the book sound a little too childish — they belong, really, to the concerns of kids younger than Jesse and Leslie — and the author herself sounds uncertain here — as if, having invented the place, she did not quite know what she wanted to do with it.

The Great Gilly Hopkins stands somewhat apart from the bulk of Katherine Paterson's work: its material is that of an old familiar genre, the problem novel. Gilly, abandoned by her mother who was a flower-power hippie in the sixties, has had a series of foster parents who cannot cope with her rebellious rudeness and generally antisocial behavior; Gilly prides herself on how brilliant she is at not getting on with her surrogate mothers and fathers and on how easily she can wreck any class at school. A severely disturbed child, one would have thought, but a weakness of the book is that she doesn't appear to be very disturbed at all: just lonely and unloved. (The same weakness appears in *The Pinballs* by Betsy Byars.) Her progress back to some kind of normality comes from her most recent foster mother — the book opens with Gilly moving into Maime Trotter's house — but not even all of Mrs. Trotter's loving kindness, it seems to me, could convert the Gilly we meet in chapter one to the girl who nurses three people through a prolonged bout of influenza, enjoys Wordsworth, and cooks a Thanksgiving dinner all on her own. It's a bit too much of a fairy tale, not in fact the reality the author thinks she is offering the reader.

Gilly is not the only weakness; Mrs. Trotter is also a figment of the imagination rather than a credible person. It isn't the caricatured, larger-than-life aspects of this physically mountainous woman that one objects to so much as the extraordinary ability she seems to have for making Gilly love her. The opening scenes — the featureless, drab house; the other foster child, a timid, pathetic little boy, William Ernest Teague; the blind black man, Mr. Randolph, who lives next door and who takes his meals with Mrs. Trotter; Mrs. Trotter herself — make Gilly feel the worst has happened to her:

> Gilly banged the door to her room for all she was worth. She spit every obscenity she'd ever heard through her teeth, but it wasn't enough. That ignorant hippopotamus! That walrus-faced imbecile! That — that — oh, the devil — Trotter wouldn't even let a drop fall from her precious William Ernest baby's nose, but she would let Gilly go to school — a new school where she didn't know anybody — looking like a scarecrow.

But towards the end of the book, when she has to leave Mrs. Trotter to live with her grandmother, she is saying:

> "Trotter! Look at me! You said you'd never let me go. I heard you." She was yelling at the totem pole

95

now. "Never! Never! Never! That's what you said!" She was on her feet stamping and screaming. The women watched her, but numbly as though she were behind glass and there was no way that they could reach in to her.

The transformation has occurred with surprising, not very credible, ease.

There are, it is true, several good points. The minor characters — William Ernest, Mr. Randolph, and Gilly's teacher, Miss Harris — are real, convincing creations; Miss Harris makes the nice observation to Gilly that "your anger is still up here on the surface where you can look it in the face, make friends with it if you want to," and the scene where William Ernest persuades Gilly to come home (she's been trying to run away and find her real mother) is well-written and moving:

> "Gilly! Gilly!" William Ernest streaked across the room and began to beat his fists on her knees. "Come home, Gilly. Please come home! Please, please!" The blood vessels stood out blue and strained on his white neck.

But the next paragraph sounds melodramatic: "The ice in her frozen brain rumbled and cracked. She stood up and took his hand." There are other moments, too, that are over-emotional, when the story comes dangerously near to being a tear-jerker. The main problem is that the author hasn't stood at a sufficient distance from her material; the skills she reveals — wit, good characterization (some of it), brief telling perceptions about life — are not sufficient to cover up this failure: both the improbability of much of the book, and the melodramatic moments are the result of a lack of objectivity.

Angels and Other Strangers is a collection of short stories, all on the theme of Christmas, that derive from tales Katherine Paterson wrote and read to the congregation of her husband's church. (He is a Presbyterian minister.) They are, on the whole, slight in subject matter, and vary in quality. The title story is the most effective: a woman runs out of gas on Christmas Eve, and is helped by a black man thumbing a lift. She is terrified of him, but he only wants a ride into Washington, D. C. He realizes her terrors, and succeeds in pacifying her; both people, before the end, show each other some Christian charity. The characters in some of the pieces are not always credible; there are, for instance, a number of children who sound like an unhappy echo of Gilly Hopkins. The situations are often rather adult, but the language throughout is simple; and though the tone is very much that of the speaking voice — these stories are obviously meant to be read aloud — the book sounds totally characteristic of the author. She manages to avoid mawkish sentimentality: by writing mostly about the lonely and the unloved she steers clear of the clichés of Christmas — cozy family reunions and eating too much. *Angels and Other Strangers* is the minor work of an important author, interesting, and a useful contribution to the literature of Christmas, but it is not Katherine Paterson at full stretch.

Jacob Have I Loved is Katherine Paterson at full stretch. It is not a flawless masterpiece; there are things in the last few chapters that strain credulity. After the hard life Louise has led in a remote fishing community — her teenage years spent in helping her father fish for oysters and crabs — it is difficult to believe that she passes her exams so effortlessly and goes off to college. Her marriage, in the concluding chapter, is also not easy to take; the whole book has appeared to be moving in another direction, preparing us to accept Louise as a woman who probably will not have a satisfactory relationship with a member of the opposite sex. There is a kind of psychological contrivance here: the story is yanked by the scruff of its neck, as it were, into a conventional ending, which, after so much excellent writing and interesting perception, makes the conclusion somewhat tame.

Once again, the book is concerned with the rejection, real or imagined, of a child by its parents. Louise's problems go right back to her birth; she is a twin, and her sister Caroline nearly died. Caroline had all the fuss and attention, but for Louise:

> My mother, seeing my distress, said, "You were a good baby, Louise. You never gave us a minute's worry." She meant it to comfort me, but it only distressed me further. Shouldn't I have been at least a minute's worry? Wasn't it all the months of worry that had made Caroline's life so dear to them all?

and, in an old snapshot:

> Caroline is tiny and exquisite, her blonde curls framing a face that is glowing with laughter, her arms outstretched to whoever is taking the picture. I am hunched there like a fat dark shadow, my eyes cut sideways toward Caroline, thumb in mouth, the pudgy hand covering most of my face.

So it continues throughout the twins' childhood and adolescence. (The parallels with another very fine young adult novel about twins, Penelope Farmer's *Year King*, are interesting — a similar exploration of jealousy, inferiority complex, and imagined rejection.) Caroline is sweet-natured, easy to please, more gifted than her sister — her parents pay for her to take piano lessons they can't afford; Captain Wallace provides the wherewithal for her to study at an expensive school of music — and finally she marries the one boy Louise really wants. It is not surprising that Louise feels left out and hurt. The kindness and affection her parents show her do not help; she can't rebel against *them*, nor against the innately good Caroline; there is no outlet for her feelings, so they turn in on herself and fester.

She takes comfort in learning how to pole a skiff, to catch crabs and oysters, cares little for her appearance, longs to be the son her father always wished for. Doing the same work as the men on the island gives her some sort of role, and she becomes an expert fisherman. It isn't the tomboy phase; its psychological roots are deeper and more complex than that, which is why the ending of the book seems contrived. During the course of the narrative, the author isn't afraid to explore the unusual. Louise at fourteen falls in love with Captain Wallace who is seventy, older than her own grandmother; it is one of the triumphs of the book that this episode is so convincing. The captain has just lost his home and all his possessions in a hurricane:

> I was terrified that I might actually see tears in his eyes and so to avoid that sight more than anything else, I slipped off the thwart, crossed the narrow space between us on my knees, and put my arms around him. The rough shirt scraped my chin, and I was aware of the pressure of his knees against my stomach.
>
> Then, suddenly, something happened. I can't explain it. I had not put my arms around someone since I was tiny. It may have been the unaccustomed closeness, I don't know. I had only meant to comfort him, but as I smelled his sweat and felt the spring of his beard against my cheek, an alarm began to clang inside my body. I went hot all over, and I could hear my heart banging to be let out of my chest. "Let go, stupid," part of me was saying, while another voice I hardly recognized was urging me to hold him tighter.

The captain never alludes to the incident, but Louise has to live with her feelings, bottling them up as usual, and when her evil-minded grandmother guesses and taunts her maliciously, she cannot answer back. Her plight is moving, her emotions entirely credible.

Jacob Have I Loved does not have a conventional narrative structure, a story with a beginning, a middle, and an end; it is, like some of the novels of Paula Fox and Jan Mark, a rich mosaic of small details, of people sharply observed, of self-contained events. It achieves a satisfying unity not just from its central character, but also from the landscape in which it is set, an island in the Chesapeake Bay: the sea, the flat marshy land, the day-to-day preoccupations, pleasures and problems of the inhabitants are revealed on almost every page of the book. The prose has a rich evocative quality that makes this background come alive:

My quiet, unassuming father, whose voice could hardly be heard in church, stood there in his oilskins, his rubber-gloved hands on his tongs, and sang to the oysters. It was a wonderful sound, deep and pure. He knew the Methodist hymn book by heart. "The crabs now, they don't crave music, but oysters," he explained shyly, "there's nothing they favor more than a purty tune." And he would serenade the oysters of Chesapeake Bay with the hymns the brothers Wesley had written to bring sinners to repentance and praise.

The incident may seem bizarre — as weird as Louise's grandmother's behavior — but the writing, expressing so well the narrator's amazement at what is happening, is extremely effective.

The characterization in *Jacob Have I Loved* is excellent: not only Louise, Caroline, and their parents; but also memorable are the minor characters, mostly oddities — Auntie Braxton with her hordes of cats, the lonely Captain Wallace who left the island as a boy in rather mysterious circumstances to return as an old man in even more mysterious circumstances, and particularly Grandma. She is an evil old woman, almost insane, constantly nagging, quoting the Bible, eaten up with jealousy and religious mania, convinced on no evidence whatsoever that Louise and her mother are whores. In her, Louise sees the dreadful effects of the limited life that a woman on the island has to lead; she must get out and find a different existence for herself as she knows she'll end up like Grandma if she does not. "Every waking moment," she says, "was poisoned by Grandma's hatred." She never answers in kind, until one late moment in the story when she gets a revenge we feel she rightly deserves:

"Here, Grandma," I said, my voice dripping molasses. "Let me help you." I'd been preparing for this moment for months. "Read it, here. Proverbs twenty-five, twenty-four." I flipped over and stuck my finger on the verse that I had memorized gleefully. " 'It is better,' " I recited piously, "'to live in a corner of the housetop than in a house with a contentious woman.'"

I smiled as sweetly as ever I knew how.

Not a perfect book, but a very fine achievement: one wonders how many more awards will come Katherine Paterson's way, for she is only now writing at her best.

References

KATHERINE PATERSON

The Sign of the Chrysanthemum Crowell 1973; Kestrel 1975
Of Nightingales That Weep Crowell 1974; Kestrel 1976
The Master Puppeteer Crowell 1975
Bridge to Terabithia Crowell 1977; Gollancz 1978
The Great Gilly Hopkins Crowell 1978; Gollancz 1979
Angels and Other Strangers Crowell 1979; as *Star of Night* Gollancz 1980
Jacob Have I Loved Crowell 1980; Gollancz 1981

BETSY BYARS

The Pinballs Harper 1977; Bodley Head 1977

PENELOPE FARMER

Year King Chatto 1977; Atheneum 1977

PHILIPPA PEARCE

A Dog So Small Constable 1961; Lippincott 1963

K. M. PEYTON

Flambards Oxford 1967; World 1968
Edge of the Cloud Oxford 1969; World 1969
Flambards in Summer Oxford 1969; World 1970

DORIS BUCHANAN SMITH

A Taste of Blackberries Harper 1973; Heinemann 1975

A Sense of Story

JOHN ROWE TOWNSEND

It is more than twenty years since the publication of *Gumble's Yard*, John Rowe Townsend's first story for children, so it may well be an appropriate time to look at his achievement so far, particularly as critical appreciations of his work have been few. This is surprising: he is a very well-known figure in the world of children's books, not only as a novelist, but as a reviewer, speaker and writer about children's literature; his assessments of other people's novels are many, but almost no one has taken a look at *his*. It may well be useful to begin with John Rowe Townsend as critic, for his work has been important and influential; indeed one could go so far as to say that few people have helped more to form prevailing taste and orthodox thinking about children's books than he has, and his works of criticism — *Written for Children* and *A Sense of Story* — show much the same characteristics as the novels.

The voice of the man and his judgments are eminently sensible, middle-of-the-road, middle-class, decent and humane; there are not many opinions in these books of criticism that most readers are likely to disagree with violently. But, conversely, there is a lack of passion, of imaginative originality. He rarely offers us anything vehement enough to make us re-examine our own views, or send us back to a neglected and underrated author, or force us to lessen our enthusiasm for one who is overpraised. Certainly there are idiosyncrasies: not many people would take K. M. Peyton as seriously as he does, nor H. F. Brinsmead. (Who? is the likely response to the mention of the latter.) But Townsend's work contains some unusual and stimulating perceptions. He is more severe than the majority of critics upon

Lucy Boston, for instance, suggesting that her real achievement is not to be found in the Green Knowe stories, but in *The Sea Egg*: this is a thoughtful and well-argued case that *does* set us wondering if he is not perhaps correct.

Written for Children — An Outline of English Language Children's Literature is, however, a very difficult book to read. The desire to include almost everybody since the eighteenth century who has written for children (except, mischievously, Enid Blyton) leaves the reader with so many hundreds of names and snap judgments that he is overwhelmed. It can only be used as a work of reference, and the trouble with this is that because so many people are included, John Rowe Townsend leaves himself insufficient space to say anything other than the bare minimum about an individual author. Nevertheless, the historical detail is erudite and accurate and his account of the changing tastes, preoccupations, and literary merit in children's literature throughout the ages is done about as well as it could be done. *A Sense of Story* is a series of essays on contemporary writers, and this format allows him more room to develop an argument, to *persuade* us rather than merely to state that *Tom's Midnight Garden*, for example, is the "single masterpiece of English children's fiction since the last war." It is a pity, however, that he takes as his assumed reader someone who, if not exactly an alien from outer space, is not widely read in the field of children's books: it means too much time is spent recounting the plots of well-known stories, as well as the adoption of a tone of voice not unlike that of a benevolent and sometimes puzzled head teacher. His comment about Ivan Southall — "I find him difficult to assess and his progress difficult to forecast" — is more of an end-of-term statement than literary criticism.

His early novels also exemplify the same virtues — decency, humanity, good sense — and the same failings — lack of imagination, of genuine originality. The first five of them, from *Gumble's Yard* (titled in America *Trouble in the Jungle*) to *Pirate's Island*, were widely praised in the sixties for their convincing characterization and their social realism: but, on re-reading them now, they seem to be particularly *un*convincing in those very departments — with the exception of the portrayal of the adults, Walter and Doris; Walter, feckless and disagreeable, and "lumpen" Doris are adults with warts, figures not often found in children's books at that time. Adventure tales of clever kids who outwit crooks, facing up to flick-knives without batting an eyelid, who burgle the big house in order to find the secret document, who get taken out to dinner by famous pop stars, have little to do with social realism; and the children themselves are not much more than stereotypes, differentiated only by standard male/female, middle class/ working class, artistic/manual, North/South interests and characteristics; none of them, with the exception perhaps of Fat Gordon, the hero of *Pirate's Island*, comes alive as an individual. Apart from Walter and Doris, the adults are rarely more than cardboard figures; Florrie, in *Hell's Edge*, is a typical example, a caricatured, generalized Northern mum:

> "Done to a turn!" she announced, beaming. "As nice a bit o' brisket as ever I saw. Now where's that lad got to? Fred, go and give our Norman a shout. Ril love, sit you down over there. Get yourself outside some Yorkshire puddin'. Build you up a bit, that will. None o' your foreign nonsense 'ere."

This is soap opera — *Coronation Street* — not social realism.

There is far too much dialogue in these novels, particularly in *The Hallersage Sound*, and too little pause for reflection, for getting inside people's feelings and thinking processes. When there is a pause — for description of scenery and place, for instance — there is again failure to make things live, to make them stand out individually:

> Though it was a clear July evening, the town lay under a faint smoky haze. It was an endless gray huddle of houses and factories, tangled tightly together. There

were hundreds of chimneys, most of them smoking. Here and there was a church spire. A murky river threaded its way through railway sidings, coal dumps, warehouses, and the black relics of Victorian industry. There were two open spaces: a football field and a cemetery.

This is Hallersage, in *Hell's Edge*, but it could just as easily be Cobchester of *Gumble's Yard* or *Widdershins Crescent;* it is a generalized description of *any* North of England industrial town.

The weakest of these stories is *The Hallersage Sound,* which seems to be little more than an attempt to cash in on the sixties pop music boom; the best is probably the first, *Gumble's Yard (Trouble in the Jungle)* which, though limited by its cops and robbers plot, does explore with some insight and sympathy the problems facing a group of children when they are abandoned by their unsatisfactory, criminal father and his selfish, sluttish girlfriend, and organize a moonlight flit to avoid being taken into care. The attempt to set up their own family unit — *The Night Swimmers* by Betsy Byars and *Fireweed* by Jill Paton Walsh, books that deal in part with a similar theme, make an interesting comparison — and look after themselves is real and harrowing. It was not until the publication of *The Intruder* eight years later in 1969, that John Rowe Townsend produced as good a book.

The plot of *The Intruder* is no more probable than any of the preceding novels and is as marred as they are by unlikely coincidences which, rather than action stemming from character, push the story on; but in most other ways it is a great advance. In young Arnold Haithwaite, Townsend creates an entirely credible and sympathetic hero — emotionally complex, intellectually slow-witted, generous but narrow; someone whom we are inside of from the beginning to the end of the book, who is changed and who grows in the course of the story. We *care* about him. (Unlike Ril Terry and Norman Clough in *The Hallersage Sound*: the reader is left there not really bothered one way or the other about whether they are likely to have a romantic relationship or not.) The author's new-found ability extends to the minor characters — Arnold's old and sick grandfather and Jane Ellison, the shy middle-class girl that Arnold fancies yet knows he can't have. Sonny — the intruder of the title, who turns out to be the real Arnold Haithwaite — is a masterly device: slimy, evil, and repulsive. And, eventually, the improbability of the plot doesn't matter, for underneath it is a much more interesting, properly worked-out story; that of Arnold coming to terms, not only with the knowledge that he is illegitimate, but that neither of his parents is a Haithwaite, that he is the result of his mother's one-night stand with a sailor from Cardiff — and that these facts are of no importance: being himself, achieving a fulfilled, adult life is what is important. Now this *is* successful realism.

The weakest aspect of the book is the background; not, this time, an industrial northern city, but a beautiful remote part of the Cumbrian seashore. It is certainly "there" as an individualized, interesting place in a way that Cobchester and Hallersage are not, but to express its power it needs a more poetic, a more sensitive pen. The opening is characteristically pedestrian:

> Sea, sand, stone, slate, sky.
>
> The village is Skirlston. The bay is Skirl Bay. The sands are Skirl Sands. The headland is Skirl Head. All take their names from the River Skirl — a short, fast-flowing stream that starts a bare ten miles away on the western slopes of the Lake District and collects a dozen other streams on its brisk way down to sea.

It's the voice of the teacher again (geography, this time), not the voice of a poet. Yet it must be said that even if he fails to bring this compelling and dramatic landscape fully to life, he does show how it moulds people: Arnold is more a product of his surroundings than of his sailor father. One is convinced that were he from somewhere else he would not be the same person. There is also some fine, dramatic tension in this book:

Arnold splashed on. Under his feet the sand crumbled and he was up to his waist. A channel. He waded. Then he was trying to climb, and step after step the bank was collapsing, letting him down again. It was like walking up a madman's staircase. Then a precarious firmness, a scramble, and the water was knee-high again. He hurried ahead as best he could. A quick look round showed Sonny, now barely visible in the gloom, but scrambling from the channel behind him.

Arnold waded another channel. The water surface swirled and eddied now as incoming and outgoing water met, danced, reared up, slid round each other. Under the surface, currents drew him all ways, nebulous arms twining round parts of his body, now gently persuading him, now jerking him viciously. For a moment his feet lost the bottom, moved sideways as if someone was trying to steal them from him. And then he was treading uphill again, was halfway out of the water.

Arnold thought he would die now. He knew Sonny would die.

Good-night, Prof, Love, (published in America as *Good Night, Prof, Dear*) indicates a further advance in John Rowe Townsend's abilities: this story of sixteen-year-old Graham falling in love with Lynn, the waitress at a local café, is for the first time totally plausible. What happens — a condemnation from Graham's stuffy parents, the young lovers running away from home, and the denouement, when Lynn telephones Graham's father to say where they are — is always credible: and, consequently, the reader's feelings are engaged from start to finish. At the time of its publication it was something of a breakthrough: no young adult novel, in Britain, had previously explored adolescent passion and sexual attraction in such depth or detail. (Ten years later, when one considers what authors have been allowed to write about since, these aspects of the book may seem a bit tame, but that is hardly Townsend's fault.) Graham and Lynn as people are convincing, and the analysis of the boy's

thought processes and feelings is particularly successful —
we really are inside both his head and his heart:

— — Hey! Graham Hollis! You left home! With her!
The enormity of it. The madness of it.

— — I know. It's mad. But.

— — They'll be after you. They'll know by now.
They'll have been up all night. Ringing the police
every half hour.

— — Oh, God. Yes. Oh, God.

— — They'll be hunting now. Police alerted. Walkie-
talkies. Missing from home in Crimley, Graham Hollis, sixteen, tall, slim, fair, may be wearing dark green
anorak. Believed to be in company of blonde girl . . .

— — Steady on. Not all *that* unusual. Not at my age.
No nation-wide search. Not like child missing on way
home from school.

— — They'll put out description, though. Tell police
everywhere.

— — Will they? Don't know what they do. *She* might
know. She's not worried, anyway. Still fast asleep.

— — They're hunting for you. You're hunted.
Wanted. Hunted. Wanted.

Less well done, however, are the other characters, who are
little more than stereotypes and the return to the author's
earlier habit of using dialogue excessively is a disappointment, indeed a considerable irritation: in order to distin-
guish who is speaking, the protagonists call each other Gray
and Lynn in almost every line, so that one is constantly
reminded that this is *not* how they would actually talk to
each other.

The Summer People is perhaps less thought-provoking
but it is a competent and interesting novel. The main
thread of its fairly complex plot is rich with possibility.
Philip and Sylvia are involved with teenagers their families
would not approve of, and they use the time they are supposed to be together seeing the girl and the boy with whom
they are really in love. Such a theme could have been

treated comically, but John Rowe Townsend takes it seriously, even solemnly, at times. The truth, inevitably, is revealed, and several people are hurt in the process. Underneath the story, which has some effective moments of drama and suspense, is a somewhat didactic parable about selfishness and lack of deep feeling. The author blames his teenagers a bit too much, perhaps; it is the class consciousness of the parents that is the main fault, but this is uneasily glossed over. As in *The Intruder*, the chief weakness is the background. The central symbol — the collapsing house on the cliffs — protrudes through the text rather obviously and, once again, the prose is too pedestrian to make the landscape — seaside Yorkshire — as dramatic as it should be. The events take place in the summer of 1939, but the imminence of the Second World War, though mentioned often enough, does not provide the tensions it should provide. Nevertheless, plot and character in this novel work very well; if not first-rate, *The Summer People* is at least a credible and satisfying story.

Forest of the Night is the first of John Rowe Townsend's books that moves away from a realistic setting. It is an attempt to use Blake's poem, "The Tyger," as a framework for an allegory about growing up and discovering one's potential, perhaps accepting one's sexuality. I say "perhaps" because it is an obscure and baffling story, a failure — pretentious and dull. It is as if the author was afraid to reveal, for some unknown reason, what he really wanted to say; the reader is left uncomfortable — as if he had intruded into someone's private nightmares. The themes and treatment need the imagination of an Alan Garner and a poet's eye for detail; Townsend has not shown such skills in this book.

Noah's Castle and *The Xanadu Manuscript* (published in America as *The Visitors*) are both concerned with the future: *Noah's Castle* is set in a not-too-distant period when society begins to disintegrate as a result of total economic collapse, and in *The Xanadu Manuscript* three people from the year 2149 are sent to investigate life in present-day

Cambridge, England. Reading these two novels after the earlier books leaves one with the impression that John Rowe Townsend decided that naturalism, for him, was a constraint and as the "realistic" people and settings are often mixed with a great deal of unlikely events, this could well be a sign that he felt that actuality was not enough. In *Noah's Castle* and *The Xanadu Manuscript*, it is as if his imagination has at last been freed, and with *Noah's Castle* he has written a fine novel. Some of the characterization may be a little thin and there is, as usual, too much dialogue, but the story — an exciting and fast-moving tale of suspense — is completely absorbing; it is not superimposed on the characters, but comes from the characters themselves as the strains and stresses of an existence in which it is almost impossible to buy food any longer begin to break up family ties and affections. Norman Mortimer — a sort of latter-day Mother Courage — is an embittered ex-army quartermaster, whose motto could be the same as Celia Withens's, "What I have I hold" in the Hallersage books. One is reminded a little of Guy Pegler in *What I Really Think of You* by M. E. Kerr. Norman loses his family, one by one, as his attempt to provide for them materially begins, more and more, to destroy his moral nature: he is an ogre who becomes, in the end, a pathetic, shrunken husk of a man. He is the most powerful and convincing character that Townsend has conceived. The tensions in the family are also done very well, often in quite simple, direct statements of complex truths. Barry, for example, is jealous that his younger brother, Geoff, is trusted by his father, whereas he is not; their sister explains:

> Someone older than Geoff might have had doubts and asked questions. Geoff hasn't reached that stage — yet.

That tells us a lot about the growing-up process and is as terse as Mary Mortimer's comment on the dullness and disappointment of her long married life:

> "He won't beat me," she said. "And apart from that there's nothing he can do to me that he hasn't done already. I haven't anything to lose."

The Xanadu Manuscript (The Visitors) is a slighter book, although it has interesting things to say on the subject of some people's inability to acknowledge the irrational and the supernatural and, by placing in the twentieth century characters who come from a society two hundred years ahead, the author is able to include some sharp observations about the advantages and disadvantages of living now. But the story lacks something: it seems to move towards moments of suspense and action, then, curiously, it hangs back: perhaps the initial idea is insufficiently developed.

In *King Creature, Come* (published in America as *The Creatures*) we are once again in the future, long after "the bad times" have destroyed civilization as we know it; humans live on, in abject urban poverty not unlike the early days of the Industrial Revolution in Britain but without any technological know-how. Beings from an alien planet have colonized part of Earth — they are called Persons; they live quite separately in their "Precinct" and regard humans as little more than animals — "Creatures" — dirty, unintelligent and contemptible. At best, Creatures can be employed as guards or garbage collectors. This background is not unlike the apartheid visions of the future in the novels of John Christopher, in particular *The White Mountains*, where catastrophe has set progress back centuries, or *The Guardians*, in which Britain is split into two halves that never meet, the Country and the Conurbs. Vector, the central character in *King Creature, Come*, is a Person, but he makes the mistake of falling in love with another Person, Melody. Persons should not fall in love, should not find each other sexually attractive — that is a disgusting attribute of a Creature. Vector and Melody leave the Precinct and go to live among the Creatures, suffering great hardship as a result or their decision.

The same theme recurs in *The Islanders*, but the setting and the plot are very different. The background here is Halcyon, a remote island in the Pacific, inhabited by a handful of men, women and children who are descendants of a ship's crew that mutinied over a hundred years previously.

This is obviously derived from the story of Fletcher Christian and the mutiny on the Bounty, but the narrative of *The Islanders* is not so much concerned with the origins of the colony as the present-day customs and behavior of the people. Their sexual morality is very strict (nudity is particularly shocking) and their religious observances are austere and puritanical. Their code of ethics is based on the Book, written by the colony's founder, who is referred to as the Deliverer; the guardian of morals, who is decision-maker in chief and clergyman, is called the Reader. In fact, he can't read, nor can any of the island's inhabitants; the teaching is handed down by word of mouth. (These structures are not unlike those of the theocratic institutions in Jan Mark's *Divide and Rule.*) When a sailor — Charlie Hewitt — arrives on the island and reads aloud to the assembled population what is written in the Book, revealing that it has almost nothing to do with what has been practiced and preached for the last century, the islanders' way of life — already beginning to change — is altered drastically.

The Islanders is a more satisfying novel than *King Creature, Come.* It has a more complex narrative, sharper characterization, a strong sense of place, and — rare in John Rowe Townsend's work — humor. There is no major flaw in the story line of *King Creature, Come;* it's clear and exciting, but the prose is a bit flat throughout and the characters unmemorable. There is nothing in it as good as some of the descriptive passages in *The Islanders:*

> All through a second night the storm roared away. And then toward dawn it stopped, so suddenly it might have been turned off by some superhuman hand. The sun came up into a silky blue sky, the wind was no more than a gentle breath, and it was summer again.

The humor comes in the person of the Reader, seventy-nine-year-old William Jonas, a delightful portrait of blinkered pomposity and absurd self-inflation:

> "Welcome to Halcyon, Mister Herrick," said the Reader the following day. "I'm glad to give you the

pleasure of meeting me. You've been a good deal in the Outside World, I hear. Well, I've met folk from the Outside World before, so you might say I'm a man of wide experience, but still, I'm very willing to meet another. And Adam here tells me you're a man of learning, too."

"I got a few books," said Charlie.

"None of 'em as big as *our* Book, I daresay," the Reader remarked. "Our Book's as long as your arm and nearly as wide as it's long."

The Islanders is John Rowe Townsend at his best, as good a novel as *Noah's Castle*. All the books from Noah's Castle onwards are concerned with people in extreme situations, with the way conventional wisdom has to adapt and change in the light of new experience. They are a far cry from *The Hallersage Sound*.

In over twenty years of writing novels, John Rowe Townsend has not given us an outstanding one. Some of his work is stimulating and exciting; it is often well-crafted and professional; but much of it lacks imaginative power and insight. He is not among the greatest contemporary writers of books for the young, though there is no denying his abilities. However, if one thinks of the many and varied aspects of his career — novelist, critic, speaker, and promoter of children's literature — his contribution is significant. He has done a great deal to raise the status of children's literature; he deserves, more than most, the Eleanor Farjeon award. One should also add that it is not every book which wins a Carnegie or a Newbery Medal that appeals widely to children. John Rowe Townsend's work is on the whole popular with young readers — he rarely forgets that the primary purpose of a novel is to *entertain*.

References
JOHN ROWE TOWNSEND
> *Gumble's Yard* Hutchinson 1961; as *Trouble in the Jungle* Lippincott 1969
> *Hell's Edge* Hutchinson 1963; Lothrop 1969

Widdershins Crescent Hutchinson 1965; as *Good-bye to the Jungle* Lippincott 1967

Written for Children Garnet Miller 1965, Lothrop 1967; revised edition Kestrel 1974; Lippincott 1975

The Hallersage Sound Hutchinson 1966

Pirate's Island Oxford 1968; Lippincott 1968

The Intruder Oxford 1969; Lippincott 1970

Good-night, Prof, Love Oxford 1970; as *Good Night, Prof, Dear* Lippincott 1971

A Sense of Story Longman 1971; Lippincott 1971; revised edition, as *A Sounding of Storytellers* Kestrel 1979; Lippincott 1979

The Summer People Oxford 1972; Lippincott 1972

Forest of the Night Oxford 1974; Lippincott 1975

Noah's Castle Oxford 1975; Lippincott 1976

The Xanadu Manuscript Oxford 1977; as *The Visitors* Lippincott 1977

King Creature, Come Oxford 1980; as *The Creatures* Lippincott 1980

The Islanders Oxford 1981; Harper 1981

WILLIAM BLAKE
"The Tyger" first published 1794

L. M. BOSTON
The Sea Egg Faber 1967; Harcourt 1967

BETSY BYARS
The Night Swimmers Delacorte 1980; Bodley Head 1980

JOHN CHRISTOPHER
The White Mountains Hamish Hamilton 1967; Macmillan, New York, 1967
The Guardians Hamish Hamilton 1970; Macmillan, New York, 1970

M. E. KERR
What I Really Think of You Harper 1982

JAN MARK
Divide and Rule Kestrel 1979; Crowell 1980

JILL PATON WALSH
Fireweed Macmillan, London, 1969; Farrar 1970

PHILIPPA PEARCE
Tom's Midnight Garden Oxford 1958; Lippincott 1959

Macho Man, British Style

Robert Westall

Robert Westall's *The Machine-Gunners* won the Carnegie Medal in 1975 which is perhaps a little surprising since in that same year Nina Bawden produced her masterpiece, *The Peppermint Pig*; but it is nonetheless a good story: amusing, exciting, with some memorably caricatured people, as salty as a seaside picture postcard.. However, the seeds of later decline were sown here, in this first novel. The plot, in the last fifty pages, becomes increasingly improbable; macho characteristics, guts rather than integrity, are extolled, and there is too much emphasis on incidents of unpleasant violence:

> Clogger raised his boot and kicked Boddser in the ribs three times. It made a terrible noise, like a butcher chopping a leg of lamb. Then he kicked him three times more, and three times more. Boddser was much more sick now. When he looked up, his eyes had changed. He looked as if he understood something he had never understood before . . .

Also the unpleasant attitudes about class (later to surface in *Fathom Five*) are already present. The paragraph in *The Machine-Gunners*, which describes the plight of a bombed-out Council House family, is an example, and one a responsible editor should have questioned:

> The family were scurrying around like ants from a broken nest, making heaps of belongings they had salvaged, and then breaking up the heaps to make new heaps. Chas watched them as if they were ants, without sympathy, because they were a slummy kind of family; a great fat woman in carpet slippers and a horde of boys of assorted sizes; hair like lavatory

brushes, coarse maroon jerseys that wouldn't fasten at the neck and boots with steel heelplates.

Not only do these attitudes become more prominent in the subsequent books, but the quality of the writing deteriorates too. The plots become increasingly thin and improbable — the supernatural elements are little more than stage props; and the characters, more often than not, are stereotypes or collections of mannerisms: one thinks particularly of Bertrand in *The Wind Eye* or Prudi, Arthur, Timmo and the two priests in *The Watch House*, or Derek in *The Devil on the Road*. The dialogue is often unconvincing — you can't create North of England speech simply by flinging the odd "bairn" or "hinny" into every third line and turning all the "I's" into "Aah's." Most irritating, too, is that Westall's writing can be garrulous, with nothing under the surface; confused by sentences in which verbs are never given a subject; marred by cliché; and hyperbolic language that is inaccurate, distasteful, or completely absurd:

> The female camp-followers had cleavages you could have ridden a horse down. *(The Devil on the Road)*

> Bertrand used the same back-handed flick to the nose. He felt the nasal bones break under his hand like Hong-Kong plastic. *(The Wind Eye)*

> I caught him smack on the nose; it made a *lovely* mess. He was a big kid; meaty slabs of yobbo muscle. *(The Devil on the Road)*

Macho attitudes increasingly replace detailed observation of the behavior of real people. Timmo's hand, in *The Watch House*, we are told "felt hard and bony and much more reassuring than Pat's. There was so much vitality in Timmo." Madeleine, in *The Watch House*, is criticized for careless driving and for being aggressive and unpleasant; whereas John, the central character of *The Devil on the Road*, who is as unpleasant and aggressive, and who drives a motor-bike far too fast, is treated very sympathetically. What is sauce for the gander is evidently not sauce for the goose. Madeleine becomes acceptable only when she re-verts to a more traditionally feminine role — happily bak-ing goodies in the kitchen. No such change occurs in John; reckless behavior on the road, violence, and rudeness are presumably virtues in men. John — with his big biceps and all the women wanting to seduce him — is more like a *Playgirl* fantasy than a real person. Girls in *The Devil on the Road* are portrayed as little more than sexual objects, and even the sprightly, forceful Johanna is most praised when most a stereotype, running around after John, cook-ing his meals, and tidying up.

Macho man is always extremely uneasy about his sex-uality and about his role in the world; machismo is a fa-çade that covers inferiority complexes of all sorts and huge chips on the shoulder. He needs to dislike a lot of things in order to reassure himself that he functions adequately, and Westall's heroes indeed dislike a wide variety of human be-havior: the upper classes, bosses of all sorts, intellectuals, university dons, middle-class people from southern Eng-land, working-class people less well off than themselves, unfeminine women, foreigners, and homosexuals. The so-cio-political attitudes expressed in *Fathom Five,* a sequel to *The Machine-Gunners,* as far as foreigners are concerned, are not far removed from those of W. E. Johns in the *Biggles* stories, with Mr. Kallonas being compared to a "Wop boxer;" the Maltese seen as criminal; and the Chinese chattering "frantically to each other like a cage of canaries." Macho man also needs to face his dislikes with an impressive show of physical force since it is usually all he has to offer. The violence in Westall's novels is particularly disturbing be-cause of the author's implied attitudes to it. Violence seems to be admired, is seen as a sign of toughness and integrity. *The Machine-Gunners,* in this respect, is every bit as bad as its successors:

> He was very silent and very hard. He was the junior
> team scrum-half and had once played a whole match

after losing two front teeth: spitting blood thoughtfully before putting the ball in the scrum, and scoring
two tries.

Thoughtfully? And consider the implications of the word
"satisfying" in this:

Clogger moved like greased lightning. His steel toecap
caught the first minion on the knee, leaving him
writhing in the gutter. His fist caught the second full
on the nose, drawing a satisfying stream of blood.

Satisfying to whom? This together with the clichéd simile
"like greased lightning" and the hackneyed "writhing in the
gutter" reduces the prose to the level of a comic or Richard
Allen's obnoxious *Skinhead*.

In *The Devil on the Road* homosexuals are insultingly
called "poufs" and are seen as predators:

Was he a pouf, getting ready to take advantage of my
drunken state? No, he wasn't a pouf. Girl like Susan
wouldn't stay married to a pouf. Besides, I wasn't the
type. Poufs like pretty-boys and I was as ugly as sin.

In an article called "Hetero, Homo, Bi or Nothing" that appeared in *Is Anyone There?* (a collection of essays and stories edited by Rosemary Sutcliff and Monica Dickens)
Westall naïvely sees homosexuals as people who listen to
Vivaldi, discuss poetry and play backgammon, while heterosexual men drink, discuss football and women. He
shows no compassion for gay people, but he expresses a lot
of sympathy for the heterosexual boy who's labelled a "pouf"
by his mates. The fear of being called a "pouf" he sees as
responsible for the lack of tenderness in young people — a
simplistic piece of reasoning by any standards.

Westall's novels certainly won't help teenagers to feel
tenderness; they're much more likely to leave young people
disturbed and uneasy. They raise to the category of virtue
far too many questionable human tendencies. John, in *The
Devil on the Road*, is one of the nastiest central characters
in recent teenage fiction, yet he's seen as a hero. He gets
very soft about cats, but never about humans. He's a rather

short-tempered, intolerant isolate who doesn't mind hitting people or dogs, even if he claims he's sorry to do so: to be sure, he is attacked by an Alsatian, but the description of his counter-attack is gloating, sick —

> I hit it a couple of left hooks, hard enough to drop any guy. No effect at all, except the sound effects of a Russian peasant being devoured by wolves. I kicked it in the guts. That discouraged it a bit, and it dropped on all fours, still having my gauntlet for breakfast. I kicked it again, in the ribs with every ounce I could put behind my Belstaff Roadrider. It made a sound like a big bass drum, and became merely one very thoughtful Alsatian. . . The middle-aged guy was worse than his dog. You know the sort: built like a Sherman tank; bald head, red face, big mouth. Kind of guy there's no point in arguing with, so you might as well just go away. He actually demanded to know why I was kicking his poor little doggy.

Westall's portrayal of relationships between men and women is often without gentleness. To macho man, women are for sex or doing the domestic chores; Johanna, John says, certainly knew how to look after her men. Macho man usually prefers talking to his own sex because it's safer, and he's more interested in proving he's as "male" as his peer-group than in entering a relationship which requires an ability to give, to love, to be tender. If Ted Hughes, in "Myth and Education" is correct in saying that great works of imaginative literature are hospitals where we heal, and that bad works of literature are battlegrounds where we get injured, then Westall's novels, particularly *The Devil on the Road*, fall into the second category.

I think a major problem with Westall's books is that the untrustworthy aliens, the chinless upper-class wets, the nagging working-class mums, the tarts with hearts of gold, the outdated slang ("jeepers") and the immature, cocking-a-snook-at-authority gleefulness of some of the attitudes, are found in TV comedy programs and old-fashioned boys' magazines, not in real life. But Westall's work is extremely fashionable, constantly praised by teachers and critics. Copies of *The Machine-Gunners* are found far more frequently in schools in Britain than any other recent novel for children set in the Second World War. Westall has also written about other things: his own work, in "The Chaos and The Track"(*Signal*); teaching English, in "The Author in the Classroom" (*The Use of English*); homosexuality, as I've already mentioned; and he is thought of by many people in the children's literature establishment as a major author. Perhaps his status has to do with what I see as defects being regarded by a great many people as real strengths. Westall must be very reassuring to the traditionalists who expect men to be tough and unsentimental, interested in motor-bikes and other suitable masculine toys; who feel women's proper place is beside the kitchen sink; who think of the Second World War as the last time "real" values were allowed proper scope; who may not object to breasts and swear-words in the teenage novel but who feel uneasy if there is any genuine exploration of teenage sexuality; who think that modern liberal tendencies are damaging the fabric of society; who regard the quality of the writing as less important than the "right" attitude.

The Scarecrows was also awarded the Carnegie Medal; Robert Westall is only the second author to have received this honor twice. It's a somber book, but, despite the illustrious award, it is not much of an improvement on its predecessors. It tells the story of Simon Wood, aged thirteen, driven almost to insanity because of the intense jealousy he feels about his mother's second marriage. He hears about a very unpleasant murder that happened a long time ago in an old mill house near where he lives, and he becomes aware of the spirits of the three people who died — the miller, his wife, and the wife's lover. The three dead people appear to him as scarecrows, and he realizes he could use them in his attempt to turn his mother against her new husband. There are clear echoes in this story of *The Owl Service* — the triangular relationship in modern times being manipulated by the triangular relationship that occurred in the past — and of *Marianne Dreams* by Catherine Storr, in which Marianne invests the stones she has drawn in her picturebook with a malevolent life of their own: they advance on the house just as Simon seems to invest the scarecrows with a kind of power, so that they also move threateningly on the house in which he lives.

There is some moderately effective writing in this novel, particularly in the descriptions of the mill and its garden:

> It was a jungle. Rose trees extended long thin branches like bending fishing rods, ten feet in the air. Laden with tiny white roses. The branches looked unsafe; waved wildly with every breath of air. There were poor grey lupins too, desperately struggling not to drown in the engulfing sea of grass. Most of the grass was dead and rotting. Dead grass thrust up through dead grass, with the living grass just managing to push out of the top, a flicker of green.

Yet there are some extremely poor passages too. As usual, Robert Westall cannot handle the big, dramatic moments except by analogy, using a cluster of uneasy similes. Here is the destruction, in the last chapter, of the mill:

> There came a crack that made him turn. Then a series of sounds like sheet lightning. A whole snapped beam of timber, sharp as a lance, speared upward through the roof, sending a patch of tiles up into the air like birds. The windows burst out in hails of shining silver like snowflakes.

Lightning, a lance, birds, snowflakes, all in five lines! And can lightning have a *sound*? Do snowflakes really look like shining silver? What, one may ask, are "hails of shining silver"? Then there is the awkward sound of "upward" too close to "up." This kind of writing is not the literary excellence one would require of a Carnegie Medal Winner.

The story itself seems to me more of an exercise in *grand guignol* than the creation of a genuinely felt experience. Also, too much is left unexplained, or seems improbable. Why do the sightseers and the TV camera crews walk so carefully around the scarecrows? How — and why — is Tris la Chard capable of seeing into Simon's mind? Why does he have such an unlikely name? (It has some resonance that is not made clear.) Tris and Simon don't always think, or speak, convincingly for thirteen-year-olds. They sound, at times, a lot older. The adults — Mum and Joe Moreton — are more real, drawn more fully.

Most of Robert Westall's prejudices are still with him. There are derogatory references in *The Scarecrows* to homosexuals and it is time someone pointed out to Westall that gays in England like being called "poufs" about as much as American blacks like being called niggers. Just as bad is the continuing obsession with class. The speech and behavior of the upper middle-class people at the art gallery preview of Joe Moreton's drawings is simply not believable; coming from the pen of an experienced author the result is embarrassing.

Of course children need to read about the nastier aspects of life: a diet of nothing but talking rabbits and Nancy Drew will equip no one for anything. But when it comes to the Second World War, rather than *The Machine-Gunners*, I would give them Nina Bawden's *Carrie's War* which stresses inner integrity, not physical prowess; and for violence, rather than *The Devil on the Road*, I would give them Leon Garfield's *Black Jack*, in which Tolly Dorking's hitherto undiscovered strengths see him through — he is a hero who is physically weak, indeed puny, but capable of really caring about people, even his enemies. For teenage relationships — loving, affectionate, sexual, considerate — those in Jill Chaney's novels are superior to almost any other author's creations, though she is totally ignored by the establishment. Her male characters are particularly successful — rounded, credible, complex human beings — too successful perhaps: they don't fit into the slots society expects. Gary in *Mottram Park*, like John in *The Devil on the Road*, is a motorcycle enthusiast, but Jill Chaney shows that owning one of these machines is not just a way of proving you're a man by charging down village main streets at eighty miles per hour.

Machismo in teenage books, it seems to me, should be recognized and deplored. An emphasis on guts, big biceps, a good fighting fist, cleavages, manly men and little feminine women, on rejecting life-styles different from the hero's or the author's just because they *are* different, is no way to help young people to be complete human beings. This emphasis does not help them to grow up; it positively hinders the process.

There are, of course, aspects of Robert Westall's work other than male machismo that may be thought worthy of comment. *The Wind Eye, The Watch House* and *The Devil on the Road* are time-slip tales with elements of the supernatural, but compared to the work of other authors in this genre — Alan Garner, Penelope Farmer, Penelope Lively — Westall's writing here, too, seems second-rate, the fantasy elements more of a vivid, theatrical backdrop than something genuinely felt and conveyed compellingly to the reader. A comparison of *The Devil on the Road* with Penelope Farmer's *Year King* is revealing; in both novels there is sex, violence, a rural setting, a male hero who owns a motorcycle, time-slip — but in every way *Year King* is the finer book, particularly in its portrayal of the central character: Lan is a complex, interesting, credible young man, not a fantasy creation of big biceps and loud mouth. Both books are in some ways inheritors of the "blood and thunder" adventure story tradition that nineteenth-century writers for young people employed so often — indeed one might say that all Westall's books follow this tradition. In the nineteenth century, too, violence was sometimes handled brilliantly, sometimes poorly — R. M. Ballantyne's *Coral Island* is an example of a book in which the author, like Westall, seems to enjoy violence, and it therefore repels the reader instead of engaging his attention. On the other hand, R. L. Stevenson in *Treasure Island* and J. Meade Falkner in *Moonfleet* create fights and scenes of danger and excitement that are totally absorbing: the blood spills and the wounds are terrible, but there is no sensational mucking about in the blood and the guts. Robert Westall could perhaps write much more persuasively if only he would stop associating such matters with spurious "manly" virtues — Stevenson and Falkner never made this mistake.

References

ROBERT WESTALL

The Machine-Gunners Macmillan, London, 1975; Greenwillow 1976

The Wind Eye Macmillan, London, 1976; Greenwillow 1977

The Watch House Macmillan, London, 1977; Greenwillow 1978

The Devil on the Road Macmillan, London, 1979; Greenwillow 1979

Fathom Five Macmillan, London, 1979; Greenwillow 1980

The Scarecrows Chatto 1981; Greenwillow 1981

"Hetero, Homo, Bi or Nothing" in *Is Anyone There?*, edited by Rosemary Sutcliff and Monica Dickens, Puffin 1979

"The Author in the Classroom" in *The Use of English,* Autumn 1979

"The Chaos and The Track" in *Signal 25,* January 1978

RICHARD ALLEN

Skinhead New English Library 1970

R. M. BALLANTYNE

Coral Island first published in 1857

NINA BAWDEN

Carrie's War Gollancz 1973; Harper 1973

The Peppermint Pig Gollancz 1975; Harper 1975

JILL CHANEY

Mottram Park Dobson 1970

J. MEADE FALKNER

Moonfleet first published in 1898

PENELOPE FARMER

Year King Chatto 1977; Atheneum 1977

LEON GARFIELD

Black Jack Longman 1968; Pantheon 1969

ALAN GARNER

The Owl Service Collins 1967; Walck 1968

TED HUGHES
    "Myth and Education" in *Children's literature in education*, March 1970

R. L. STEVENSON
    Treasure Island first published in 1883

CATHERINE STORR
    Marianne Dreams Faber 1958; in America as *The Magic Drawing Pencil*, A. S. Barnes 1960

Macho Man, American Style

S. E. HINTON

The two most remarkable aspects of S. E. Hinton's books are that they are written by a woman and that they are widely read, praised, and recommended by an establishment one imagines would be the most likely to condemn them. Her output is small. Her first novel, apparently inspired by social injustices at her high school in Tulsa, Oklahoma, was *The Outsiders*, published in 1967, and it was written when she was only sixteen. This was followed by *That Was Then, This Is Now* in 1971, *Rumble Fish* in 1975 and *Tex* in 1979. It is easy to see why her work would be liked by many in their early teens, particularly boys, but it is hard to fathom the reasons why she has won critical acclaim, and why so many copies of her stories are found in classroom libraries. *The Outsiders* is an extremely unusual achievement for a sixteen-year-old, and it may well be that critics, astonished that she could have done it at all, have been excessive in their praises. *That Was Then, This Is Now* and *Rumble Fish* are, in fact, much the same book as their predecessor. The characters may have different names, but they are similar stereotypes; the language, the first-person narration, the events, the attitudes are more or less identical. The writer's concerns, vision, and language, show almost no variation or development.

If one did not know that S. E. Hinton was a woman, it would be difficult to deduce this fact from reading her novels. Girls, in her world, rarely figure as major characters; it is an almost entirely male-dominated scene, set in deprived working class areas where delinquent and semi-delinquent boys continually fight each other to prove who is boss or who has the biggest muscles or just for the sake of fighting.

Girls are "chicks" — not much more than status symbols — important only as possessions, along with cigarettes, liquor, cars, and the hardware used in a rumble. Adults are mostly absent, and when they do appear they are usually ineffective, weak creatures who have long since given up the struggle. The attitude to women is that of patronizing male superiority:

> "That's funny," I said. "Chicks crying bore me. Go on Mike, finish your story." (*That Was Then, This Is Now*)

> Pretty little thing, she looked like a dandelion with her hair messed up. (*Rumble Fish*)

> I couldn't see what messing around with a chick at the lake had to do with me and Patty. It didn't have anything to do with me and Patty. Why would she let something stupid like that louse us up? (*Rumble Fish*)

> She wriggled in my arms like a landed bass. (*Tex*)

It is a common enough phenomenon that some boys, particularly at the "gang" phase of their lives, are so unsure of themselves that the only people whose reactions they value are those of their peers, or other males slightly older; the relationships of any real importance at this stage are often with someone of their own sex. Girls, therefore, are seen as inferior creatures, or something to acquire and show off to other boys; they are not seen as human beings. It isn't that S. E. Hinton is inaccurate here. The problem is that there is no voice in her novels other than that of the teenage narrator; she seems to make no value judgments, so that all too frequently she appears to be condoning attitudes that are adolescent, generally anti-social, and sometimes immoral.

It is hard for an adult to feel much compassion for her characters and it's difficult to care about what happens to them. The texture of the books is so thin; we really are enclosed in a world of immaturity. Even the names of the characters are unlikely — Sodapop, Ponyboy, the Motorcycle Boy, Two-bit, and so on. They are names out of the imaginary worlds, the fantasies of teenage boys, not those of living people. *The Outsiders* is largely concerned with warfare between the "Socs" and the "greasers," gangs that are divided on class lines, but it's unusual, somewhat unlikely, that kids from affluent families would go around trying to beat up other groups of adolescents. Ponyboy, the narrator, is the youngest of three brothers in a parentless family; despite the delinquent tendencies of this trio, the constant fighting, the tacit approval of criminal activities — "He could lift a hubcap quicker and more quietly than anyone in the neighborhood" — we are asked to see them as paragons of almost every virtue:

> He has Dad's eyes, but Soda is one of a kind. He can get drunk in a drag race or dancing without ever getting near alcohol. In our neighborhood it's rare to find a kid who doesn't drink once in a while. But Soda never touches a drop — he doesn't need to. He gets drunk on just plain living. And he understands everybody.

The Motorcycle Boy, in *Rumble Fish*, is shot dead by the police shortly after stealing some fish from a pet shop; he's a crazy, mixed-up delinquent, but the way he talks suggests a rather more reflective and sensitive person than he actually is:

> "It's a bit of a burden to be Robin Hood, Jesse James and the Pied Piper."

And

> "California," he said, "is like a beautiful wild kid on heroin, high as a kite and thinking she's on top of the world, not knowing she's dying, not believing it even if you show her the marks."

Fighting occurs and recurs every few pages. Some teenage boys will enjoy this; it appears to give approval to some of their less pleasant tendencies. There is nothing here for the adult; maybe because S. E. Hinton fails to convince the reader of the reality of her world. In my view, a good young adult book, a good children's book, is simply a good book:

it can interest readers of all ages. The young don't inhabit a different planet. They are of our planet, and we are of theirs. This kind of thing has no interest for anyone except the teenage boy:

> Just like I expected, he tried to make the most of that moment, lunging at me. I was quick enough, though, grabbing the chain, dodging the knife, and sticking out my foot to trip him. He just stumbled, and whirled around, jabbing at me. I sucked in my gut and wrapped the chain around his neck, jerking him to the ground. All I wanted to do was get the knife away from him. I'd kill him later. First things first. I jumped on top of him, caught his arm as he swung the knife at me, and for what seemed like hours we wrestled for that knife. I took a risk I thought was worth taking and tried holding his knife hand with one arm, and used the other to smash his face. It worked, he loosened his hold on the knife long enough for me to get it away from him. It fell a few feet away from us, far enough away that I didn't bother trying to reach out for it, which was good. If I had gotten a hold of it, I'd have killed Biff. As it was, I was pounding his brains out. (*Rumble Fish*)

Clichés: "lunging," "whirled around," "what seemed like hours," "pounding his brains out," "first things first;" the clumsy repetition of "away" three times in fourteen words and "knife" six times in the whole passage; the unreal, detached tone as if the protagonist was a distant observer: Where is the fear? The pain? A fight like this, if convincingly written, should disgust the reader. Not make him yawn. (The killing of a cat in Susan Cooper's *Dawn of Fear*, for instance, is done with more emotional force than any of S. E. Hinton's fights between humans.)

As I said before, a viewpoint other than that of the narrator is needed, because we are offered so many attitudes we want to reject:

> He stole things and sold them, or stole them and kept them, or stole things and gave them away. It didn't

bother me. He was too smart to get caught. He had
been stealing things since he was six years old. I wasn't
above taking a pack of cigarettes from a drugstore, but
that was about it. I was the hustler and Mark was the
thief. We were a great pair. (*That Was Then, This Is
Now*)

The narrator, admittedly, goes on to say that he thinks
stealing is wrong, though he qualifies this with "or at least
against the law;" but on the whole theft is seen here as
wholesome entertainment. "We were a great pair." "He was
too smart to get caught." The Robin Hood touch is meant
to make it more palatable — "he stole things and gave them
away." "I wasn't above taking a pack of cigarettes" implies
that it is peculiar *not* to do so. The dangerous aspect of this
is that immature readers will absorb the immoral and anti-
social attitudes, not see them as wrong, and glorify them
into something acceptable. So why is S. E. Hinton praised
by critics, used in school by teachers? Because they know
this will appeal to kids who read, and be the hook to lure
kids who are non-readers? Is it a soft option then, bait to
persuade people to read — easier stuff to use than more
"literary" young adult fiction?

That Was Then, This Is Now is marginally more interesting than *The Outsiders* or *Rumble Fish*. There is a
mildly interesting central relationship, and an awareness of
change in feelings and attitudes as the teenage years move
on. Bryon and Mark are not related, but they have been
brought up by the same mother so that they are virtually
brothers and very close friends. The book charts the course
of their drifting apart as Bryon, weary of the gangs and the
fights, settles down to a steady affair with a girl and attempts to find a job. Mark moves the other way, into the
drug scene. Bryon no longer needs his "brother" when he
starts to get serious about Cathy, one of the few girls in
S. E. Hinton's novels who is something more than a
shadow. But he still sees Mark as "a dangerous, golden lion"

— a literary phrase, in the bad sense of the term, inconsistent with the narrator's usual English — to stand between him and the world:

> Mark was acting strange these days, too. He would stare at me for long periods of time when he thought I wasn't watching, like he was trying to find the old Bryon in this stranger, like he was trying to figure out who I was. One night he even almost lost his temper with me when I told him I was goofing around with Cathy instead of with him. It was as if he felt something slipping and was trying to hang on.

When Bryon discovers that Mark is a drug pusher, and could therefore be responsible for the acid trips that have almost destroyed Cathy's young brother, he informs the police. Mark is tried and sent to jail. The relationship is finished. When Bryon visits him in the penitentiary, Mark says:

> "I didn't have to see you. I wanted to, though. I had to make sure."
> "Make sure of what?"
> "Make sure I hated you."

He adds, later in the conversation, "When I get outa here, you ain't never going to see me again." At about the same time, Bryon breaks off his affair with Cathy, for somewhat obscure reasons — he doesn't love her any more, it seems, because of what he's done to Mark — and he is left at the end of the story with nothing at all. The last words are: "Me, once I had all the answers. I wish I was a kid again, when I had all the answers." Part of the growing up process is the discovery that many of the major questions in life don't have obvious answers, but it is rather depressing to find that the central character wishes to turn the clock back instead of moving on.

The setting of *That Was Then, This Is Now* is the late sixties, the hippy, flower-power era — better done, in fact, in Paul Zindel's *I Never Loved Your Mind*. At least the book, by implication, takes a firm attitude against the sale and use of drugs; for once the author's moral stance is clear.

Drugs aren't seen as similar to stealing, something about which ambivalent attitudes — "at least it's against the law" qualifying "I still felt that stealing was wrong" — are in any way tenable. Moral stance is cloudier in *Rumble Fish* and *The Outsiders*, but drugs and flower-power hippies do not figure in either book.

Rumble Fish has a brief portrait of one of the few adults in S. E. Hinton's novels. Rusty-James's father is a wino who neglects his children and has not a care in the world about what they do or what happens to them. We're told — it sounds unlikely, considering the working-class attitudes and language of Rusty-James himself — that he was "a practitioner of the law." He comments on his family:

> "Your mother," he said distinctly, "is not crazy. Neither, contrary to popular belief, is your brother. He is merely miscast in a play. He would have made a perfect knight, in a different century, or a very good pagan prince in a time of heroes. He was born in the wrong era, on the wrong side of the river, with the ability to do anything and finding nothing he wants to do."

This implies that we have no capacity to overcome the problems of our birth and upbringing, no free will; it is "the stars, the stars above us, govern our conditions." Rusty-James, at the climax of the story, sees his brother killed by the police, then slashes his wrists on the broken glass of the police car window, and later gets "dried out" in a reformatory. He hasn't moved on; he remains crushed by what has occurred:

> "I figured if I didn't see him, I'd start forgetting again. But it's been taking me longer than I thought it would."

He is, therefore, in much the same frame of mind as his father, feeling he has no ability to control his fate. It is another very depressing conclusion. *Rumble Fish* is a fairly tedious book: One cannot like or approve of the central character and his family, so it is difficult to become involved or feel sympathetic. The one fairly "good" guy is

Steve, Rusty-James's best friend, but as we see him only through Rusty-James's eyes, he comes over as a weak, dispiriting person. It is, mercifully, a very short novel.

The Outsiders is about twice as long; it has a greater degree of complexity and makes some attempt at a coherent narrative. The main weakness of the story is that the action and the characters strain credulity too much and too often. In a fight with the "Socs," Ponyboy's friend, Johnny, kills Bob with a knife. He and Ponyboy give up their prized "greaser" hairstyles (this seems to bother them more than Bob's death) and hide in a deserted old church. Here, Ponyboy recites Robert Frost when he sees the dawn rise, and reads most of *Gone With the Wind*! They are obviously going to be caught eventually, but the scene of their undoing is also somewhat implausible. A school party arrives for a picnic; the church catches on fire, becomes a blazing inferno within seconds, and Johnny, Ponyboy, and a friend of theirs, Dally, who has come to see how they're getting on, help to rescue the kids. Johnny later dies of his burns in a hospital — presumably, as he's the boy who killed someone, he has to be dispensed with, but trial and juvenile detention would not do as he's supposed to be a "nice" guy. Ponyboy then writes the whole of *The Outsiders* — the retelling of these events — as an assignment for his English teacher.

It is not easy to take such a scenario very seriously. A semi-delinquent thirteen-year-old, a "greaser," parentless, living a rough life in a house with no adults, reciting poetry and writing a novel? Improbable, to say the least. Johnny, we're told, was like "a little dark puppy that has been kicked too many times and is lost in a crowd of strangers;" he

> had a nervous, suspicious look in his eyes, and that
> beating he got from the Socs didn't help matters. He
> was the gang's pet, everyone's kid brother. His father
> was always beating him up, and his mother ignored
> him, except when she was hacked off at something,
> and then you could hear her yelling at him clear down

at our house . . . He would have run away a million times if we hadn't been there.

This boy, when dying, writes a letter to Ponyboy with this kind of insight and poetry:

I've been thinking about . . . that poem, that guy that wrote it, he meant you're gold when you're a kid, like green. When you're a kid everything's new, dawn. It's just when you get used to everything that it's day. Like the way you dig sunsets, Pony. That's gold. Keep that way, it's a good way to be.

This isn't realism. It's fantasy, in the worst sense of the word. These books may have been inspired by the author's anger at social injustice, but the end products are not believable stories about real people. The characters are either incredible or unsympathetic, the action often repetitive, the implied attitudes questionable. The teenage reader may like them, but they are not good literature in any sense of that term.

Tex stands apart from the other three novels in a number of ways. There is, it is true, the same tone of voice, and the same first-person narration, which, as usual, means a constant abuse of the English language: "like" for "as," "laying" for "lying," et cetera. (A review in *The School Library Journal* said of *Rumble Fish* that it was "stylistically superb" — a very peculiar judgment.) But Tex McCormick, the main character, is undoubtedly much more real than anyone in the other three books — a rounded, convincing portrait of a boy who is finding his adolescence very hard going. Clumsy, unsure of himself, physically stronger than he realizes, reacting in all the wrong ways to the problems he encounters, he emerges as a complex human being. The reader, for once, is involved, and begins to care about what happens. The setting, too, is different: Tex lives out in the country and trips to the city are infrequent; city life he regards with a sort of gauche wonder. It's unfortunate that there is almost no description of the landscape — we could, as usual, be almost anywhere — but there is a little more awareness of surroundings than in the previous novels:

> This was the first day I could really feel fall coming
> on, not so much because it was chilly, but there was
> a slant to the sunlight and a smell in the air that
> meant fall.

The story is virtually plotless. It consists of a number of
self-contained incidents that happen to Tex at the end of
his fourteenth and the beginning of his fifteenth year. The
unifying factors are Tex himself, and the changing pattern
of his relationships with his elder brother, Mason, who is
seventeen, and his friends and neighbors, the Collins family. Tex and Mason have no mother, and Pop is mostly absent. (When he does appear, he makes more of an
impression on the reader than the vague ciphers that pass
for adults in the previous books.) The two brothers, therefore, have to deal with many situations that are beyond the
normal scope of teenagers, but one of the faults of the story
is that they sound much older than they really are; Mason,
in particular, reacts and behaves like an adult in his mid-
twenties. Tex at fourteen seems to have no problems in
driving a car, says things like "I'd never been drunk before.
I know that's hard to believe, me being so close to fifteen
years old, but it was the truth," deals effectively with some
drug pushers by waving a gun at them, and has insights
beyond his age and experience: "There was something about
him hurting like that and being too proud to say anything
that really made me sad." Here is Tex, driving a pick-up
truck and coping with a hitchhiker who has just stuck a
gun in brother Mason's ribs:

> The hitchhiker turned to look. I put my foot on the
> brake and tried shoving it through the floor. I spun the
> steering wheel like it belonged to a boat instead of a
> car. The truck whirled around and slid like a panicked
> horse. It skidded across the road and teetered on the
> edge of the ditch for what seemed like an hour; every
> single thing that had ever happened to me flashed
> across the windshield like a movie. It almost turned
> over, then rocked to a slanted standstill, half in the

ditch. The hitchhiker slung open the door and leaped out before we stopped moving.

Improbable, to say the least, that a fourteen-year-old would react so coolly. Every image that illustrates every idea is a cliché: there is an excess of similes — "what seemed like an hour," et cetera. This is a writer whose work has been called stylistically superb! But the events of the book, on the whole, *are* probable, at least until the last few chapters. That Tex, in one day, should discover he and Mason are only half-brothers, deal with the drug pushers, and end up in hospital with a shot-gun wound, is straining credulity just as much as the way he dealt with the hitchhiker.

Tex is the only one of the four novels in which there is a strong portrait of a girl. Tex falls in love with Jamie, the youngest member of the Collins family; the course of their relationship, the different hopes and demands each has of the other, the antagonism mixed up with the attraction, are all well done — undoubtedly the best part of the book. Jamie is no stooge or acquisition to show off, like the girls in *The Outsiders*. She is determined, individual, and speaks her mind. One good scene shows her taking chauvinist Lem Peters down a peg or two; Lem's wife has just had their first baby and Jamie asks if it is a boy or a girl:

> "A boy," Lem said proudly.
> "Yeah?" said Jamie. "Well, don't worry. If it'd been a girl you could have just tried again until you got what you wanted."

"I don't think you two could raise a cat," she tells him, and says she knows all about discrimination: "look who has a motorcycle and who doesn't." It is good to see that S. E. Hinton *can* create a female character with the ability to disturb the pretensions of male superiority which fill up most of the pages of her books, even if Jamie, like Tex and Mason, sounds older than she is. (She's fourteen.)

The macho, more male-than-thou adult or teenager is a bore, whether he is met in real life or in the pages of a novel. But considering the development *Tex* shows, as compared with the previous books, there is perhaps a ray of hope that S. E. Hinton will write about characters that are complex and interesting, about teenagers who do have parents, and who do something other than smoke, drink, and fight. Maybe, too, she will find a voice that will make her dull, one-dimensional prose style more memorable, but that does not seem so likely.

References

S. E. HINTON

The Outsiders Viking 1967; Gollancz 1970
That Was Then, This Is Now Viking 1971; Gollancz 1971
Rumble Fish Delacorte 1975; Gollancz 1976
Tex Delacorte 1979; Gollancz 1980

SUSAN COOPER

Dawn of Fear Harcourt 1970; Chatto 1972

MARGARET MITCHELL

Gone with the Wind Macmillan, New York, 1936; Macmillan, London, 1936

PAUL ZINDEL

I Never Loved Your Mind Harper 1970; Bodley Head 1971

Beyond the Last Visible Dog

RUSSELL HOBAN

Russell Hoban is the author of several novels for adults, one full-length story published on a children's list (*The Mouse and His Child*), and for more than twenty years he has been the writer of texts of picturebooks for young readers. It is the last-named area that he would probably regard as the measure of his contribution to children's literature, for *The Mouse and His Child* was written for adult publication and only became a juvenile by accident.

A number of changes have taken place over the past two decades in the world of picturebooks, the most interesting being the advances made in the reproduction of artwork in color, and the fact that many artists who, a quarter of a century ago, would have been regarded as decorators of other people's work, now write and illustrate their own stories. A picturebook these days can be a beautiful object, a work of art in its own right: the subservience of the illustrator to the author is no longer considered a necessity; he doesn't exist merely to render in visual terms another person's words. It is possible now — and it happens occasionally — for the words to be subservient to the pictures, indeed to be almost irrelevant. Some of the productions of Brian Wildsmith, for instance, seem like glossy coffee-table books for the young — striking and original pictures occupying most of the available space, with an odd word or two at the foot of the page. *The Haunted House* by Jan Pienkowski was not intended to have a text at all; it was added at the last moment to avoid a curious state of affairs in the United Kingdom's taxation laws — books there are not subjected to Value Added Tax; but *The Haunted House*, a pop-up, would be regarded by the Inland Revenue as a toy if it had no words, and toys *are* subject to V.A.T.

Good artists are not automatically good writers, however. John Burningham's work is a constant pleasure to the
eye, but the stories that accompany his pictures can be thin;
the well-known *Mr. Gumpy's Outing*, for example, is not
particularly memorable in its choice of words, and its narrative is somewhat predictable. Charles Keeping, perhaps
more interested in words than John Burningham, also does
not always succeed in writing a story that is as convincing
as the dazzling colored pictures that he paints. *Charlie,
Charlotte and the Golden Canary*, for instance, is marred
by a rather sentimental story line. There are some artists,
however, who do solve the problem brilliantly. Ezra Jack
Keats is one, and Maurice Sendak is probably the supreme
example: the narrative structure and the way the pictures
convey the emotions within the words in *Where the Wild
Things Are* and *In the Night Kitchen* could hardly be bet-
tered, whatever strange judgments may be made about
them by adults who fear that toddlers will be frightened or
disturbed. (In my experience, no child I've come across has
been alarmed by monsters in *Where the Wild Things Are*,
nor upset by nudity in *In the Night Kitchen*; adult hang-
ups are the voice behind such reservations.)

Russell Hoban began his career as an artist. He attended
the Philadelphia Museum School of Industrial Art, and
later, after working as the television art director in a big
advertising agency, he became a free-lance artist. But it is
not as a painter and illustrator that he is known. Soon after
he established himself as a writer of picturebooks, he gave
up the idea of wishing to illustrate them; the early *What
Does It Do and How Does It Work?* — not a story but an
explanatory text about power shovels and dump trucks —
shows that a considerable talent in picturebook illustration
has disappeared from children's literature. For many years
the illustrator of his stories was his first wife, Lillian, but
recently a number of different artists, both British and
American, including Quentin Blake and Emily Arnold
McCully, have illustrated his work.

The writing in Russell Hoban's picturebooks has changed and developed greatly over the years. The earlier books for the most part contain realistic narratives — some of them rather didactic in intention — whereas the more recent ones can be wildly fantastic, showing vivid and bizarre flights of imagination and a delicious sense of humor. Even the seven very popular Frances books are more concerned with teaching something to the child reader than in telling a story for its own sake. Frances — indeed all the characters — are badgers, but their behavior is entirely middle class. To all intents and purposes Frances is a little girl who has to learn a series of lessons — how to cope with jealousy on her younger sister's birthday (*A Birthday for Frances*), how to outwit false friends (*A Bargain for Frances*), or how to make real friends (*Best Friends for Frances*). Parents and teachers no doubt like these tales because they are useful. That is a perfectly proper function of some books, some people think, but it is only a secondary function. Story is more important, and story in the Frances tales, though suited to the pre-school intentions of the books, is not always particularly interesting:

> It was a pleasant summer morning, so Frances took her bat and her ball and some chocolate sandwich cookies and went outside. "Will you play ball with me?" Frances's little sister called to her as she was leaving. "No," said Frances. "You are too little." Gloria sat down on the back steps and cried. (*Best Friends for Frances*)

Frances has to discover how to find room in her games for her little sister, not just on those occasions when there is no one else to play with, but also when she wants to play with badgers of her own age. In the end she is happy to do so:

> "It was only yesterday that you got to be big enough to play baseball. But I will give you half the daisies Albert gave me." So Frances gave Gloria half the daisies, and Gloria stopped crying. Then Harold came over, and everybody played baseball — Gloria too.

The lessons Frances learns are those the vast majority of children need to learn; yet one can have picturebooks that are not only didactic, but put forward the wrong kind of lesson. Russell Hoban's *Tom and the Two Handles* seems to me to be a little dubious in its morality. Tom's friend Kenny gives him a bloody nose, but when he tells his father he's going to get his own back by doing the same thing in return, Dad says they ought to talk it over and become friends again. Kenny punches Tom a second, a third, a fourth time; so Dad decides to teach Tom how to fight. Eventually —

> "Well," said Tom, "after I gave Kenny a bloody nose, I knocked him down. Then I sat on top of him. And I told him there was more than one way of looking at it. I told him that he could say I gave him a bloody nose. Or he could say that he had a bad time with his best friend and we could make up. So we made up."

Dad approves of all this, but I'm not sure that I think it's a good — or, indeed, a likely — way of helping a shaky friendship to become whole.

As soon as the need to teach disappears from Russell Hoban's texts, the writing improves. One notices it even in books he had published at the same time as the Frances stories: it is as if he is released from some kind of unwelcome pressure; the prose becomes more flowing, more sure of itself. The cadences are more musical, and there is room for humor and for making the reader enjoy turning the page to find out what happens. *Ugly Bird* appeared in the same year as *Best Friends for Frances* and it's a much better book. Again, it is worthwhile quoting the opening sentences to see the difference:

> Once there was a very ugly bird baby, and his mama loved him. But all the other birds said, "My goodness, what a very ugly bird baby that is!"
>
> "Never mind," said Mama to her baby as she petted him. "They just don't know."
>
> "Don't know what?" said the ugly bird baby.

> "Don't know who you are and what you are," said
> Mama.
> "Who am I and what am I?" said Baby.
> "When it's flying time we'll both find out," said
> Mama. "Eat your worm and grow."

Baby does find out, in a pleasingly unpredictable way, who
he is and what he is, but the really imaginative surprises
and delights come in the later books, particularly *Arthur's
New Power*, *The Twenty-Elephant Restaurant*, and *How
Tom Beat Captain Najork and His Hired Sportsmen*. *Arthur's New Power* is a joky, satirical piece about domestic
electrical gadgets that become substitutes for conversation
and the finer things of life; Father Crocodile comes home
one evening to find his house in darkness because his wife,
son, and daughter have used too much power:

> "While she was ironing, she was watching the Early
> Horror on TV," said Arthur, "plus wearing her Slimmo
> Electronic Wonder-Massage belt and listening to her
> stereo with headphones. If you unplugged Emma, she
> wouldn't know what to do."
> "What about Mom?" said Emma. "She was plugged
> into her bio-feedback machine, listening to her alpha
> waves and watching the yoga lady on the kitchen TV
> and mixing kelp-and-carrot cocktails in the blender."
> "You see what I mean?" said Arthur. "And everybody
> yells at me for plugging in one little amplifier."

This is all the funnier when one remembers that these are
crocodiles talking! Quite gratuitously they are crocodiles —
they could just as easily be hippopotamuses or boa constrictors — but the fact that they are crocodiles seems to
add an extra touch of craziness to the story.

The plot of *The Twenty-Elephant Restaurant* is even
more bizarre. A man and a woman are fed up with their
dining room table being wobbly, so the man makes a new
one steady as a rock; "elephants could dance on that table,"
he says. In his wife's reply lies the nature of the book's ludicrous humor: she takes his image as literal, and asks,

"How many?" They discuss how many and advertise in the paper — "Elephants wanted for table work. Must be agile." Eventually they open a restaurant with twenty tables; on each one is a full-size dancing elephant. The business is a huge success, but after a while the dancing tilts the foundation of the building, so they move on with their elephants to a new site and stay there until *that* building is also disturbed. And so on: it has the possibility of as many repetitions as the Last Visible Dog in *The Mouse and His Child* — the label on a tin of dog food has a picture of a dog and a tin of dog food; on the latter is a label with a dog and a tin of dog food: et cetera. The humor reminds one of the work of the Absurdist drama of the 1950s and 1960s — Ionesco's *Rhinoceros*, N. F. Simpson's *One-Way Pendulum*, or some of the situations in the plays of Samuel Beckett. It doesn't, of course, have the same profundity or the same pretensions; it's just a crazy flight of fancy for kids. And adults.

The finest of all these picturebooks is the most well-known of all — *How Tom Beat Captain Najork and His Hired Sportsmen*. This story had some rather curious origins. The organizers of the Exeter, England conference on children's books in 1972, asked Russell Hoban to write something that could be used as the basis for an exercise in mime, movement, and dance. He sent them *How Tom Beat Captain Najork and His Hired Sportsmen*, then existing only in typescript; so its first admirers were not readers but an audience watching a performance. Several eminent children's writers, publishers, and librarians played the parts, a somewhat bewildered but most convincing Brian Alderson taking the role of Captain Najork. Later the book was published with the superbly effective Quentin Blake pictures. Every sentence in this story is a gem:

> "Very well," said Aunt Fidget Wonkham-Strong at table in her iron hat. "Eat your greasy bloaters."

> Tom took his boat and pedalled to the next town down the river. There he advertised in the newspaper for a new aunt.

or

> The hired sportsmen brought out the ramp, the slide, the barrel, the bobble, the sneeding tongs, the bar and the grapples. Tom saw at once that sneedball was like several kinds of fooling around that he was particularly good at.

The plot tells us how Tom's aunt, annoyed that her nephew does nothing but fool around, sends for Captain Najork to teach him a lesson by beating him at fooling-around games. But the Captain loses every time, and Tom leaves to find a new aunt, Bundlejoy Cosysweet. "She had a floppy hat with flowers on it. She had long, long hair." He tells her his conditions — no greasy bloaters, no cabbage-and-potato sog. And he does lots of fooling around. "That sounds fine to me," she says. "We'll have a go." The captain marries Aunt Fidget Wonkham-Strong, so they all live happily ever after.

Underneath this dotty and enchanting story lie some serious themes — childhood innocence pitted against adult incomprehension; repressed adults disliking nonconformity; a genuine aunt not necessarily being a blood relative. The child reader will not, of course, be aware of any of this, but, as Ted Hughes said in "Myth and Education," literature for the young is often a blueprint or do-it-yourself kit for experiences that children cannot yet have the equipment for dealing with in real life. Since they may absorb ideas subconsciously, it is very important to consider what kind of experiences we want them to encounter when they read a book. The underlying themes of *How Tom Beat Captain Najork and His Hired Sportsmen* are far more worthwhile than those of, say, *Tom and the Two Handles*, just as the idea behind *Where the Wild Things Are* is valuable in its suggestion that fear is more to do with what is going on inside us rather than what is outside us: much more therapeutic than a conventional story of beasts and monsters.

Picturebooks at their best should put us in touch with as universally interesting matters as any of the major novels we may read in the years of our maturity.

Russell Hoban did not write *The Mouse and His Child* with a young audience in mind; it was intended to be a novel for adults. His publisher, however, decided to issue it as a children's book as it is a story about talking animals and toys. It's impossible, of course, to know precisely what alterations, if any, were asked for when the publisher decided to place this novel on a children's list, but the adult reader may well wonder how a seven-year-old can deal with some of the difficulties it presents:

> "The upside-downness of self," said the voice. "A good beginning. Continue."
>
> "We cannot continue," said the father, "unless we are put back on dry land and wound up."
>
> " 'Wound up?' " said the voice. "Define your terms."
>
> "I don't want to," said the father. "I don't like this sort of talk."
>
> "What other sort of talk is there?" said the voice. "Here below the surface one studies the depths of TO BE, as manifest in AM, IS and ARE. And if you don't hold up your end of the conversation I may very well snap you in two even though I don't choose to eat you."

The influence of Lewis Carroll is obvious here, as it is in other parts of the story; other influences elsewhere in the writing are Hans Andersen and Samuel Beckett, the latter a particularly unusual person to see lurking behind the pages of a so-called children's book.

Maybe the difficulties shouldn't worry us: there is much here that a child can enjoy, the ideas and the pace of the narrative, for instance. It's a "chase" plot, the villain pursuing the good characters through a series of dangerous situations, until the concluding chapters when the individuals with whom we identify — the mouse and his child — win out, and the baddie, Manny the rat, is rendered powerless. This is a common enough story line in scores of children's books. The mouse and his child are wind-up toys, thrown out with the garbage when they are broken. Manny, the boss of the town's dump, repairs them and forces them to work for him, but with the aid of an old fortune-telling frog, they escape. Manny vows revenge and sets off in pursuit, declaring that he will smash them to bits with a large rock. The mouse and his child, helped by the frog, a kingfisher, a friendly bittern and a clockwork elephant, defeat the rat and his allies in a full-scale battle: Manny's teeth are knocked out so he is now useless as a leader. He starts working for the mouse and his child, but his wicked nature is untamed — he has a complex plan to electrocute his enemies, which, happily, fails.

Manny is an interesting villain:

> A large rat crept out of the shadows of the girders into the light of the overhead lamps, and stood up suddenly on his hind legs before the mouse and his child. He wore a greasy scrap of silk paisley tied with a dirty string in the manner of a dressing gown, and he smelled of darkness, of stale and moldy things, and garbage. He was there all at once and with a look of tenure, as if he had been waiting always just beyond their field of vision, and once let in would never go away.

But he is not wholly evil; in some ways he is pleasant and amusing, and capable of having his better nature appealed to, not unlike the ambiguous figure cut by Long John Silver in Stevenson's *Treasure Island*:

> The house, he saw, had not burned down, and he found that he was glad. "Say vat again," he murmured faintly.
>
> "Say what?" asked the mouse child.
>
> "What you called me," said Manny Rat.
>
> "Uncle Manny?"
>
> Manny Rat nodded, and smiled a toothless smile, and felt the darkness that dwelt in him open to the light.

The reader, towards the end, feels that the author is becoming more interested in Manny than in the mouse and his child, rather as Milton in *Paradise Lost* found Satan more interesting to write about than God; this impression is confirmed by the fact that Russell Hoban at one time planned a sequel, called *The Return of Manny Rat*. This exists only as a fragment: it describes how Manny gets a new set of teeth made of papier mâché, gnaws his way into a church, finds himself completely baffled by the organ — he thinks the stops are door-knockers, and wonders what sort of creature Diapason is — and experiences the greatest moments of his whole life when he hears the organist play Bach's Passacaglia and Fugue in C minor. Maybe there wasn't a possible narrative to develop, but it is a pity that this extremely amusing piece, though published, remains unfinished.

The influence of Hans Andersen makes itself felt particularly in the opening chapter of *The Mouse and His Child* — the toyshop with the toys that speak after midnight, Christmas, snow — and the effect is almost like a Christmas card in words:

> The sound of music made him stop at a toyshop where the door, continually swinging open and shut in a moving stream of people, jangled its bell and sent warm air and Christmas carols out into the street. "Deck the halls with boughs of holly," sang the loudspeakers in the shop, and the tramp smelled Christmas in the pine wreaths, in the bright paint and varnish, in the shining metal and fresh pasteboard of the new toys.

Russell Hoban often uses Christmas as a background — *The Mole Family's Christmas* and *Emmet Otter's Jug-Band Christmas* are picturebook stories set at this time of the year. The author, like Katherine Paterson in *Angels and Other Strangers*, employs the season of good will to emphasize the loneliness of certain individuals. It is a recurring theme in his work; father-son relationships are also a recurring theme — they are at the center of *The Mouse and His*

Child and also his novel for adults, *The Lion of Boaz-Jachin and Jachin-Boaz*. Much of the time the mouse and his child are friendless, vulnerable, indeed pitiable in their inability to help themselves. Russell Hoban seems to have a particular interest in a child's loneliness and naïveté — the big outside world is awesome and frightening in its complexity. *Ugly Bird*, for instance, also touches on these ideas.

The major problem confronting the mouse and his child is movement. They can only dance in a circle, and when Manny repairs them, they are able to travel only in one direction, the father walking forward, holding up his child at arm's length, and the child cannot look at what is ahead of the father. Their greatest wish is to be self-winding, so that they can deal with life more easily, and it is Manny, eventually, who gives them this ability. The limitations on movement are reminiscent of ideas in the plays of Samuel Beckett — in *End Game*, Clov can only hop, and Hamm can only move when Clov pushes his wheelchair; in *Happy Days*, Winnie is buried in the first act up to her waist in a mound of sand, in the second up to her neck; in *Play* the three characters are incarcerated in urns and can only move their heads. The mouse and his child spend several months upside down in mud at the bottom of a river, and when Serpentina the turtle turns them the right way up, they still cannot move. The play — The Last Visible Dog — presented by the amateur theater group, the Caws of Art, seems particularly close to Beckett; in it Furza and Wurza live in tin cans half buried in mud, just as the legless Nagg and Nell in *End Game* live in trash-cans at the front of the stage. The Caws of Art is one of the areas of the novel that is above the head of the young reader — it is a wickedly funny parody of a second-rate experimental drama group that has lost any real rapport with its audience:

> "Out among the out among the out among the dots."
> After which Crow stepped out of his role and said, "You feel it building?"
> "No," said Mrs. Crow. "I'll be honest with you. I don't feel it building."

"Never mind," said Crow. "Just let it happen. Your line."

"Where among the dots?" said Mrs. Crow.

"Out among the dots beyond . . ."

"Yes, yes. Go on. Beyond?"

"Beyond the . . ."

"Don't stop now. . . . Beyond the . . .?"

"BEYOND THE LAST VISIBLE DOG!" shouted Crow. "There!" he said to his wife. "See how it pays off? Up and up and up, and then Zonk! BEYOND THE LAST VISIBLE DOG!"

"It's getting to me now," said Mrs. Crow. "But what does it mean?"

Crow flung wide his broad wings like a black cloak. "What *doesn't* it mean!" he said. "There's no end to it — it just goes on and on until it means anything and everything, depending on who you are and what your last visible dog is."

" 'Beyond the last visible dog,' " said the mouse child to his father. "Where is that, I wonder?"

"I don't know," said the father, "but those words touch something in me — something half remembered, half forgotten — that escapes me just as it seems almost clear."

Difficult also for the young reader is the distressing scene in which the shrews attack and kill another colony of shrews; they in turn are eaten by the weasels who are promptly slaughtered by an owl. This may be unpleasant, but only temporarily; we are not asked to be directly involved with the shrews, the weasels, or the owl, who are essentially minor characters, and in any case animals eating each other is a fact of life that a child has to learn to accept:

Behind them on the snow lay fallen shrews and wood mice, their open mouths still shaping final cries of rage and fear, their open eyes fast glazing in the moonlight. The mouse child stared beyond his father's shoulder at the astonishing stillness of the dead. The father looked at the spears he carried; he had felt the weight of enemies upon them, and for the first time in his life knew what it was to strike a blow for freedom.

It was a good decision to publish *The Mouse and His Child* as a book for the young reader; it is a fine work, entertaining and thought-provoking. The qualities of its writing are outstanding, particularly the sensitive descriptions of nature:

> Winter had left the pond. The trees had lost their bare sharpness, and their branches were blurring into leaf. Skunk cabbages pushed their coarse green points up out of the black, boggy earth, and the nights grew clamorous with spring peepers. Robins were hard at work among the earthworms; the rattling cry of the kingfisher sounded along the banks; mallards cruised among the reeds; and from the surrounding swamps came the whistle of the marsh hawk and the pumping of the bittern. The fish that swam past the mouse and his child moved more swiftly now, and the sunlight filtering through the depths seemed warmer than before. Grown frogs and young tadpoles, newts, snakes, and turtles, awakening from hibernation, swam up to the surface as spring came to the pond.

This compares very favorably with the famous description of spring in the concluding pages of E. B. White's *Charlotte's Web*. *The Mouse and His Child* thoroughly deserves the status it has achieved as something of a modern classic in children's fiction. No doubt there will be many more picturebooks to come from Russell Hoban, but one hopes that he will also give us another full-length novel: it's long overdue.

References

RUSSELL HOBAN

What Does It Do and How Does It Work? Harper 1959
Tom and the Two Handles Harper 1965; World's Work 1966
The Mouse and His Child Harper 1967; Faber 1969

A Birthday for Frances Harper 1968; Faber 1970
Best Friends for Frances Harper 1969; Faber 1971
Ugly Bird Macmillan, New York, 1969
The Mole Family's Christmas Parents 1969; Cape 1973
A Bargain for Frances Harper 1970; World's Work 1971
"The Return of Manny Rat" in "Thoughts on a Shirtless Cyclist, Robin Hood, Johann Sebastian Bach and One or Two Other Things" in *Children's literature in education*, March 1971
Emmet Otter's Jug-Band Christmas Parents 1971; World's Work 1971
The Lion of Boaz-Jachin and Jachin-Boaz Stein & Day 1973; Cape 1973
How Tom Beat Captain Najork and His Hired Sportsmen Atheneum 1974; Cape 1974
Arthur's New Power Crowell 1978; Gollancz 1980
The Twenty-Elephant Restaurant Atheneum 1978; Cape 1980

SAMUEL BECKETT
End Game Faber 1958; Grove 1958
Happy Days Faber 1961; Grove 1961
Play Faber 1968

JOHN BURNINGHAM
Mr. Gumpy's Outing Cape 1970; Holt 1971

TED HUGHES
"Myth and Education" in *Children's literature in education*, March 1970

EUGENE IONESCO
Rhinoceros French & Eur 1959; French 1959

CHARLES KEEPING
Charlie, Charlotte, and the Golden Canary Oxford 1967; Watts 1968

JOHN MILTON
Paradise Lost first published in 1667

KATHERINE PATERSON
Angels and Other Strangers Crowell 1979; as *Star of Night*, Gollancz 1981

JAN PIENKOWSKI
The Haunted House Heinemann 1979; Dutton 1979

MAURICE SENDAK
Where the Wild Things Are Harper 1963; Bodley Head 1967
In the Night Kitchen Harper 1970; Bodley Head 1971

N. F. SIMPSON
   One-Way Pendulum Faber 1961; Grove 1961
ROBERT LOUIS STEVENSON
   Treasure Island first published 1883
E. B. WHITE
   Charlotte's Web Harper 1952; Hamish Hamilton 1952

Plums and Roughage

PETER DICKINSON

"The danger of living in a golden age of children's literature is that not enough rubbish is being produced," Peter Dickinson wrote in an article entitled "A Defence of Rubbish." This stimulating and provocative piece also contained such challenging statements as "Nobody who has not written comic strips can really understand the phrase economy of words. It's like trying to write *Paradise Lost* in haiku," and "I am fairly sure . . . . that a diet of plums is bad for you, and that any rational reading system needs to include a considerable amount of pap or roughage." Many characteristics of Peter Dickinson the novelist are reflected in these remarks — the humor, the use of epigram, the suggestion that he doesn't want the reader to accept him as being totally serious even if he is saying something that is essentially truthful. There is in all his books a sense of ambiguity in what he hopes the reader's response will be: "I'm supplying roughage," he seems to be hinting, "but there are quite a few plums if you care to search for them;" or, in other words, the novel to Peter Dickinson is, before anything else, *entertainment* — improbability, the far-fetched or the psychologically unlikely character or event don't matter that much if the narrative excitement sweeps the reader along. Messages, fine writing, original and profound comments about human behavior may well be there too, but they are perhaps secondary in importance to holding the reader in the spell of an enthralling story.

The refusal to take himself absolutely seriously is both a strength and a weakness. His decision not to use the Byzantine background, for instance, of *The Dancing Bear* as an opportunity to lecture the reader on that period's art and culture provides an interesting contrast to the approach of Jill Paton Walsh, in *The Emperor's Winding Sheet*, in which she also used that civilization as material for a novel, albeit a different period of the Eastern Roman Empire's history. I am not suggesting that *The Emperor's Winding Sheet* is a less effective achievement; Jill Paton Walsh's concern that the reader should master the historical detail leads to some impressive and absorbing writing. Peter Dickinson, quite unworried about authentic historical detail, provides instead an equally convincing narrative that works very differently: some of *The Dancing Bear*'s best sequences are to do with marauding Huns, about whom, he tells us in his prefatory note to the book, very little is known. "I've invented a lot of details," he says, and "I'm not ashamed of these inventions." In his essay "The Day of the Tennis Rabbit," he confesses that the portrayal of daily monastic life in Eastern Tibet in *Tulku* was entirely his own invention, because nothing is actually known of what went on in Tibetan monasteries at the beginning of the twentieth century. Not taking himself seriously, however, is a weakness in other books. *The Weathermonger*, for instance, shows a modern Britain turning its back on technology and reverting to the Middle Ages, but this is used merely as colorful background material to the narrative which is essentially about something else: kids outwitting adults. The opportunity to explore the Luddite mentality is to a large extent lost: the resonances with Charlotte Brontë's *Shirley* or John Christopher's *The White Mountains* are missing, and the explanation for what has happened — that an eccentric Welsh pharmacist has accidentally discovered the tomb of Merlin and brought him back to life, and that it is Merlin's distaste for machines which is causing people to smash them up — seems at best unlikely, at worst trivial or childish.

There are plenty of plums, as I said, in the roughage, though that varies from one novel to another; it almost seems to be deliberate, for there is no sense that the serious elements in the novels increase with each succeeding one, or that success means Peter Dickinson feels he has to take himself more solemnly in *The Seventh Raven* than he did in *The Weathermonger*. *The Blue Hawk*, which has the most plums, is followed by *Annerton Pit* which is largely, though not wholly, roughage. The adult literary critic will naturally prefer the plums; I doubt if *The Blue Hawk* — Peter Dickinson's most impressive book, winner of the Guardian Award and perhaps more deserving of the Carnegie Medal than *Tulku*, which received the medal in 1980, and *City of Gold and Other Stories from The Old Testament*, the 1981 winner — is as widely read by children as *Annerton Pit*. (Peter Dickinson is, incidentally, the only writer to have won the Carnegie Medal two years running.) *Tulku*, perhaps more than any other of his novels, is the richest Peter Dickinson "mix" — the one that most obviously reveals his strong points and his limitations — and is worth considering in some detail.

Tulku has a gripping narrative. It begins in China; the period is the Boxer Rebellion, and in the first chapter all the inhabitants of a Christian village are slaughtered except for one boy, Theodore, the thirteen-year-old son of the settlement's founder, an American missionary. Fleeing the place, Theodore meets Mrs. Jones, an eccentric English botanist who finds time between shooting bandits to stop and paint wild flowers, and her Chinese servant, Lung, who becomes her lover. This strange trio, after many exciting adventures, make their way into Tibet, where, helped by a lama who thinks the pregnant Mrs. Jones is to give birth to the new Tulku (the future chief lama), they stay for months in a monastery. Eventually Theodore makes his way through India to Britain and home to America. Wildly improbable though this scenario is, Peter Dickinson's immense skill in unfolding an absorbing story holds the reader from beginning to end. One of the strengths of the book is that none of the main characters is required to do any heroic, larger-than-life deeds that seem beyond their capabilities and experience — a fault that hurts the credibility of *Heartsease, Emma Tupper's Diary, The Gift*, and *Annerton*

Pit. The Tibetan background is also well described, though the real "plum" of the book is the widening of Theodore's religious experience — this is the main theme of *Tulku*, an exploration of the nature of religious belief. (It is also the main theme of *The Blue Hawk*.) Theodore's brand of Christianity is narrow, thou-shalt-not puritan Protestantism; he is therefore initially very shocked by Mrs. Jones's propensity to swear, the "immorality" of her relationship with Lung, and the heathen practices of the Tibetan monks. He gradually realizes that the swearing is more a manner of speech than genuine profanity; that the sexual sinfulness of Lung and Mrs. Jones is unimportant compared with their love for each other; and that the heathen customs do not imply a denial of God. Peter Dickinson presents the religious ceremonies as if they are meaningless mumbo-jumbo and a possible cover-up for a political power-struggle going on in the monastery (the parallel with *The Blue Hawk* is striking); but, he tells us, the presence of God *is* here: it is up to each individual to discover that in his own particular way —

> The Lama, explaining what he meant by saying that Mrs. Jones had not needed to understand her initiation ceremony, but only to have faith in it, had told the following story: some three hundred years before, the fifth Dalai Lama had noticed the goddess Tara walking every day along the pilgrims' path round his palace. He made enquiries and found that one old man among the pilgrims made that journey every day, repeating the mantra wrong each time, so the Dalai had him taught the correct words. Immediately the goddess ceased to walk the pilgrims' way, and did not reappear until the old man was allowed to say her mantra in his old, meaningless way. Theodore hated this story but couldn't forget it. It embodied so much he disliked and distrusted about the Lama's religion — the empty repetition of syllables, like the automatic rotation of prayer-wheels, as if nonsense was more

holy, more worthwhile, than honest, wholesome intelligence striving for the meaning of things . . . and yet at the same time Theodore himself acknowledged a presence that listened morning and evening to his attempts to pray but gave no other sign.

Throughout *Tulku* the writing is excellent; there are a great many telling phrases and striking images. The destruction of the Christian settlement as if "the wheel of a passing cart had rolled across and demolished it into mere sand" is not only an impressive metaphor but an ironic use of the word "wheel" — to Westerners an object that is merely useful (and at times, therefore, dangerous), to Tibetans a religious symbol. In Tibet no wheel would crush anything; wheels are forbidden to have any utilitarian function. A felicitous employment of irony is also shown in the description of Theodore's father as "an athlete of faith, funnelling all his energies into his worship, consciously driving himself on to further attainments and endurances;" and ironic, too, is the moment when Theodore first sees Lung not as a servant but a person in his own right: Lung was "not just an animated bit of Mrs. Jones's baggage." The jolting juxtaposition of Christian boy and Buddhist monastery is most effectively conveyed in passages like this:

Theodore had his ladder up against the idol of the Buddha and was using a soft brush to dust among the crannies of an intricate jewelled shoulder-piece when it struck him what a contrast this was with the almost appalling smoothness of the face. He paused and looked up. This particular statue had the eyes closed in contemplation, but from where he was standing on the ladder Theodore could see that the lids were not completely shut, and that through the slit between them and the gold underlid Someone might be watching him.

As if to prove that the face was nothing but gold and stone, Theodore climbed the last two rungs and deliberately scuffed the dust from its smile. He had been going to rootle with his brush into the inch-wide nostrils, but suddenly he felt ashamed and returned to the jewelled shoulder-piece. The gesture seemed to have worked, and the idol was inanimate once more.

The faults of *Tulku* are as striking as its strengths, however. Theodore never, in his speech, sounds like an American; he often thinks and acts as if he is older than he really is and it is impossible to believe that a child whose whole way of life is extinguished in a moment, whose father is killed, would be so psychologically unbattered. Mrs. Jones — a sort of British Mae West, warm, vulgar, and invulnerable — is, initially, quite credible; her cool in the face of danger is engaging and probable, but her conversion to Buddhism is extremely unlikely and her Cockney speech throughout unreal: stage Cockney. With such weaknesses in the two main characters, it is a remarkable achievement to leave the reader feeling that he has experienced something so intelligent and enjoyable. *Tulku* is a first-rate yarn. It's very superior roughage; in other words, excellent entertainment. There is nothing reprehensible in that.

The Blue Hawk is the only novel of Peter Dickinson's that is free of any kind of improbability. Maybe its setting, in an unnamed place and time, possibly on another planet in some distant part of the universe — the same device used by Jan Mark in *Divide and Rule* and *Aquarius* — frees Peter Dickinson from the restraints of a realistic framework; but, granted that, this imaginary country has to obey its own logic, and it does, impeccably, throughout. The message — that true spirituality is found within, not in the observance of religious rituals — is the same as in *Tulku*; here it is discovered by the central character, Tron, another young adolescent, who, almost from birth, has spent his life in the temple and its precincts training to be a priest. Tron, at the beginning of the novel, appears therefore to be little more than a human robot; any original quirks of thought and feeling should have been suppressed so that he

PETER DICKINSON

can be a little cog in the temple's vast machine of ceremonies and observances. On the day of the ritual reconsecration of the king, however, he is Goat — allowed for twenty-four hours to act on any impulse. The ceremony revolves round the sacrifice of a blue hawk: Tron picks up the hawk before it is killed and walks out of the temple with it, thus proving that all those years of training haven't quite destroyed his natural feelings and the ability to think for himself. The consequences of this action are, apparently, calamitous. The king is murdered and Tron's life is in danger. But he is befriended by the king's son, and he slowly comes to realize that a tremendous power-struggle is going on between the new king and the priests for control of the government of the country. As in *Divide and Rule*, the priests alter the ceremonies and their meanings to suit their own ends, but Tron is not Hanno. He is an opposite type of person, in fact — not, as Hanno is, broken by the ruling theocracy because he can't control his natural, unthinking animal self. Using the self-discipline he has learned as a novice priest, Tron helps to break the power of the theocracy, and, in so doing, discovers within himself his long-suppressed spontaneous nature and a genuine spirituality. Despite the obvious similarities between *The Blue Hawk* and *Divide and Rule*, the intentions and achievements of the two authors are quite different. Unlike Peter Dickinson, Jan Mark has no religious message to impart; she is more interested in showing how the powers of an establishment destroy outsiders and misfits, how the person who cannot bend or pretend becomes the victim. Peter Dickinson is more concerned with showing that evil can be overcome by intelligence, cunning, and courage. Both writers, however, seem to be saying that when religious organizations become politically powerful, like the Papacy in medieval times for example, corruption is inevitable; spirituality dies, ends justify means, and religion becomes a grotesque travesty of its original intentions. The Keeper of the Rods says to Tron

> ... if I miss one small motion prescribed by the rules, that error will do more than repeat and repeat itself year by year. It will cause other errors, which will also repeat themselves and also cause further errors, so that in a very few years the Rack of Days would lose all meaning ... You think a little change here and there will do no harm? ... Very soon men would be trying to change the Gods.

The ponderous writing rather cleverly suggests a ticking clock — it also shows some influence of the slow, measured tone of voice of Ursula Le Guin in *A Wizard of Earthsea*. The Keeper of the Rods is talking about the instruments he uses to measure time, but he is quite unwittingly making a comment about what has happened — how the country's religious hierarchy has become totally perverted. As in *Tulku*, irony in *The Blue Hawk* is a very effective device.

The intellectual content of Peter Dickinson's other novels is less exacting than in *The Blue Hawk*; but *The Seventh Raven*, quite different in theme, style, and atmosphere from any other of Peter Dickinson's books — there is enormous variety in his work — makes a number of serious statements about politics and art. Mrs. Dunnitt says (it is almost the same as the central theme of M. E. Kerr's novel, *Gentlehands*)

> .... There are professional torturers in the world who go home from their ghastly work like a man going home from his office, and they kiss their wives and read a bedtime story to their children and after supper they put on a record of the Mozart Requiem and listen to it with real appreciation. Art is no salvation. Art is no excuse.

and

> Our country, and others like it, is run with the prime object of making you and me comfortable. In the days of the cave-men we would have been the ones with places close to the fire. As it is, we are the ones who

have the cottages in Wales and the Volvos and the private education for our children and the index-linked salaries and pensions. But we are not fools. And we have consciences. We can see that our privileges need to be justified.

The plot of *The Seventh Raven* is concerned with the attempts of a group of South American terrorists to kidnap the son of their country's ambassador to Britain; they are amateurs at the job, however, and they unintentionally find they are having to hold as hostages a hundred children who are rehearsing an opera in a London church. Hostage literature is topical — inevitably — and there are now several good novels on this theme in children's and young adult fiction; *The Siege of Babylon* by Farrukh Dhondy and *Hostage!* by James Hamilton-Paterson are excellent examples, though the best of the genre is Robert Cormier's *After the First Death*. *The Seventh Raven* has a narrative as exciting and tightly knit as *After the First Death*, characterization as convincing as that in *The Siege of Babylon* and *Hostage!*, but it is weak on probability; the way the siege of the church ends is a happy coincidence, and the improvised trial staged by the terrorists is not the most likely thing they would do in the circumstances. But this novel has several notable marks of originality. The skill with which the author handles a huge cast of characters is admirable. The first-person narration, by an upper-class girl, is excellent; her tone of voice and all the slang, the idioms, the emphatic adjectives — "ghastly," "beastly," " super," "frightful" — that someone from such a background would use, ring true throughout. It's a remarkably different style of writing from any other that Peter Dickinson has used and it never falters. Interesting parallels are drawn between acts of terrorism, political demonstrations, plays in the theater, trials in courts of justice, and the opera in the church; they are neatly summed up by Mrs. Dunnitt as —

All gestures . . . Often a gesture is the only action you can take, you know. That's how I came to be interested in costumes.

In 1979 people in Britain stayed indoors to watch the siege of the Iranian Embassy in London "as if it were almost a play," the narrator comments. The girl terrorist is acting a part; she

> was standing with her right hand on her hip and her left foot planted a little forward. Her face was set like a mask and she stared out over our heads. It was a pose, an attitude struck on purpose, as if she'd been modelling for a photograph — guerilla chic, I thought, but I expect in her own mind she was posing for the statue of liberation they were going to put up in the main square of San Matteo.

The distinctions between life and art, reality and illusion, Peter Dickinson is saying, become blurred at certain times, particularly in times of violence and danger. It is an almost Pirandellian proposition, thoughtful and teasing. *The Seventh Raven* is, once again, first-rate roughage with some excellent plums, less yarn than *Tulku*, more approachable than *The Blue Hawk*, but not one hundred per cent convincing. *After the First Death* as an exploration of the kidnapper/hostage situation, is a finer book, presenting the reader with a story that seems less contrived.

Peter Dickinson's first three novels, *The Weathermonger*, *Heartsease*, and *The Devil's Children*, are all set in Britain at a time when machines have been smashed, when thousands of people have fled to the continent of Europe to escape the collective madness of returning to a rural existence without any kind of scientific know-how. *The Weathermonger* and *Heartsease* have exciting adventure narratives, but they are marred by the fact that the child protagonists are required to be mentally and physically tough, quick-witted, ingenious, and devious to an unbelievable degree. The characterization, too, is weak — most of the children are unmemorable, two-dimensional creations. *Heartsease*, however, has some fine descriptive passages:

> . . . every breath she took was full of the odour of new growth, a smell as strong as hyacinths. In winter there

are no smells, or very few and sour — woodsmoke and reeking dung heaps and the sharp odours man makes with his toil. There comes a morning when the wind is right and the sun has real pith in it, and then all the sappy smells of growth are sucked out of the earth, like mists from a marsh, and the winds spread them abroad, streaming on the breeze with a thrilling honey-sweetness which even high summer — the summer of bees nosing into lime-blossoms — cannot equal.

The Devil's Children is the most successful of this trio of novels. The story is more plausible, the characterization subtler, and its theme — race relations — very well handled. Nicky, the main character, has lost her parents in the mad stampede to leave England when "The Changes" came; she is befriended by a large family of Sikhs who walk out of London and settle in a country village where they earn their living as blacksmiths. At first the hostile, racially prejudiced villagers don't want to have dealings with the Sikhs at all; "the Devil's children" they call them, but Nicky acts as the go-between who persuades them to buy the tools and implements they need. The portrayal of the Sikhs' way of life, their customs and family relationships, is sympathetic and convincing; the irrational attitudes of the villagers also come over with considerable power. "They had built up," Nicky realizes, "a whole network of myths and imaginings around the Sikhs," one story of which is that they may be descendants of "the Queer Folk," smiths and ironworkers who used to "live under the hills" — in other words, pixies or leprechauns. Nicky, too, is regarded with deep suspicion —

> They stopped looking at her in the face when they spoke to her, as though they were afraid of some power that might rest in her eye. Also, if there were children in the Borough when she came past, mothers' voices would yell a warning and little legs would scuttle for doorways. Once Nicky even saw a soapy arm reach through a window and grab a baby by the leg from where it was sleeping in a sort of wooden pram.

The Sikhs have their own stereotypical notions too. Jamaican bus drivers, they imagine, drink all night; the British in India "would go and admire the Taj Mahal, but all the time they were thinking about drains." This, of course, makes the Sikhs seem all the more human — they have no monopoly on being right every time. *The Devil's Children* is one of the most thoughtful discussions of racial intolerance in contemporary children's literature, almost as good as James Vance Marshall's *Walkabout* and Mildred Taylor's *Roll of Thunder, Hear My Cry*.

The successful handling of the theme of racism is all the more interesting when one considers that elsewhere in Peter Dickinson's work there are a number of (presumably) unconscious racist put-downs. The Chinese and the Tibetans in *Tulku* at times seem to be regarded as second-class citizens; the Scots in *Emma Tupper's Diary* are often seen as joke figures in kilts and sporrans; and Greeks, we are told in *The Dancing Bear*, "will always choose to argue about an action as a substitute for doing it." The Italian Mr. Palozzi in *The Gift* is a dreadful example of racial stereotyping. When his daughter says she loves Mr. Venn, "Mr. Palozzi was furious and began shouting about the honor of the family and sharpening an old bayonet he happened to have" —

> "When I am young," muttered Mr. Palozzi, "I have eight sisters. They sleep in one room, and in that room they have one picture on the wall. One picture of the Holy Virgin. Right? Now I have one daughter, and she has on her wall not eight pictures — no — eighty. Eighty different men! I am disgusted!"

This is viewing Italians as little more than "I eata-da-spaghetti" comics. *The Gift*, in fact, is a moderately interesting novel about a boy who has the ability to see into other people's minds; the tension of the narrative comes from his detection, by this means, of a violent psychopathic killer who is involved in a payroll snatch at a nearby building site. I say only moderately interesting because the final confrontation between Davy and the psychopath is poorly done (Davy acting out of character as if he were an experienced adult psychiatrist, not a child), and there is little that is of high quality in the dialogue or the characterization. There is a carelessness about the writing in this book, as if the author was not fully engaged with the subject, or maybe it is a sign of the weakness inherent in not taking himself seriously enough. The same can be said of *Emma Tupper's Diary* and *Annerton Pit*, although both these novels have some aspects of interest. The narrative of *Emma Tupper's Diary* has an original and intriguing idea — when some teenagers who live near a Scottish loch decide to bring a little amusement and perhaps money into their lives by faking a monster (thus diverting the media's attention away from Loch Ness), they discover some *real* prehistoric monsters in their loch — but the characterization is either dull or improbable, the conservationist message of the conclusion hammered home unsubtly, and, once again, the protagonists perform colossal feats of endurance without batting an eyelid. The latter fault also spoils a great deal of the widely read and much acclaimed *Annerton Pit*. The portrayal of the central character's blindness is excellent; and so is the description, the feel, of the deserted coal mine where over a hundred men, women, and children died in an explosion in the nineteenth century. One of the points that the author wishes to make — that certain places where terrible disasters have occurred seem haunted by fear and evil for ever — comes over most convincingly. But the unbelievable sang-froid of the blind boy, Jake, in situation after situation, the insipid depiction of his elder brother and his grandfather, and the involvement in the narrative of a group of ecology-inspired terrorists, suggest that the serious themes of the book (fear, blindness, the far-reaching consequences of appalling calamities) are unhappily married to the rather stale, conventional themes of a standard kids' adventure story.

Finally, it is perhaps worth returning to *The Dancing Bear* — like *Tulku* a historical romance — to quote from Peter Dickinson's writing at its best. In this novel he is not failing by trying to do too many things at once, or being slapdash with characterization and dialogue; the book's two great strengths — the sweep of the narrative that impels the reader along, and the power of the prose — make it only slightly less of an achievement than *The Blue Hawk*. (The missing element is a certain seriousness of purpose.)

> Silvester looked back and saw the people jostling over the bridge and round the gate; slowly, like sand going through the neck of an hourglass, the crowd became smaller as it pushed through the little wicket, each man too anxious to make his escape inside to stop and open the main gate for others. The enormous walls stood solid on either side, looking as though they could hold the City alone, without the help of sol-diers; but the ease with which the rabble had broken through made Silvester see how thin they really were — like the shell of a crab, a little brittle bone guarding all the rich meat within.

The crab and the hourglass images are splendidly accurate.

Peter Dickinson is prolific, imaginative, and resourceful. Not many contemporary writers of children's fiction show such variety of theme and treatment — each new book of his invariably strikes the reader as unpredictable, a pleas-ant surprise. And when it comes, ultimately, to separating the roughage from the plums, much of the roughage is of superior quality. It certainly isn't *rubbish*.

References

PETER DICKINSON

> *The Weathermonger* Gollancz 1968; Atlantic/Little, Brown 1969
>
> *Heartsease* Gollancz 1969; Atlantic/Little, Brown 1969
>
> *The Devil's Children* Gollancz 1970; Atlantic/Little, Brown 1970
>
> "A Defence of Rubbish" in *Children's literature in education* 3, November 1970
>
> *Emma Tupper's Diary* Gollancz 1971; Atlantic/Little, Brown 1971
>
> *The Dancing Bear* Gollancz 1972; Atlantic/Little, Brown 1973

The Gift Gollancz 1973; Atlantic/Little, Brown 1974
The Blue Hawk Gollancz 1976; Atlantic/Little, Brown 1976
Annerton Pit Gollancz 1977; Atlantic/Little, Brown 1977
Tulku Gollancz 1979; Dutton 1979
City of Gold and Other Stories from The Old Testament Gollancz 1980; Pantheon 1980
The Seventh Raven Gollancz 1981; Dutton 1981
"The Day of the Tennis Rabbit" in *The Quarterly Journal of the Library of Congress*, Fall 1981

CHARLOTTE BRONTË
Shirley first published in 1849

JOHN CHRISTOPHER
The White Mountains Hamish Hamilton 1967; Macmillan, New York, 1967

ROBERT CORMIER
After the First Death Pantheon 1979; Gollancz 1979

FARRUKH DHONDY
The Siege of Babylon Macmillan, London, 1978

JAMES HAMILTON-PATERSON
Hostage! Gollancz 1978; Philomel 1980

M. E. KERR
Gentlehands Harper 1978

URSULA LE GUIN
A Wizard of Earthsea Parnassus 1968; Gollancz 1971

JAN MARK
Divide and Rule Kestrel 1979; Crowell 1979
Aquarius Kestrel 1982

JOHN MILTON
Paradise Lost first published in 1667

JILL PATON WALSH
The Emperor's Winding Sheet Macmillan, London, 1974; Farrar 1974

MIILDRED TAYLOR
Roll of Thunder, Hear My Cry Dial 1976; Gollancz 1977

JAMES VANCE MARSHALL
Walkabout Michael Joseph 1959; Morrow 1959

Long Ride Through a Painted Desert

Virginia Hamilton

There is no doubt that Virginia Hamilton can write: as a painter of landscape or the creator of the apposite image and the memorably concise perception, only Paula Fox, Betsy Byars and Ursula Le Guin are her rivals among contemporary American writers of fiction for children. But the journey from *Zeely* to *Sweet Whispers, Brother Rush*, to borrow a phrase used twice in *Arilla Sun Down*, is "a long ride through a painted desert." Only two of her nine novels — *Zeely* and *M.C. Higgins, the Great* — are one hundred per cent successful, though *Sweet Whispers, Brother Rush* has some fine passages; in all the others there is some major flaw that spoils the finished product. In *The House of Dies Drear* and *The Planet of Junior Brown* it is credibility: the reader cannot believe in the reality of events and people; these two books are fantasies, not reflections of deeply felt life. In *Arilla Sun Down* and *Justice and Her Brothers* there are too many words and not enough space between the words: narrative is slow to the point, at times, of tedium; page after page of descriptive prose with very little dialogue leaves the characters seen dimly, as if through a fog. The last two stories of the Justice trilogy, *Dustland* and *The Gathering*, suffer — as do some of Peter Dickinson's books — from too much concentration on technological paraphernalia; the characters do not develop, so their reactions and thought processes become predictable. The writing from *Arilla Sun Down* onwards is at times unnecessarily obscure or so fussy with detail that it acts as a barrier between the reader and the material; a child in particular may well give up the struggle:

> "Hur'm up, Strider!" Softly Run. Run making a squeaking with his mouth. Strider rushing into the wind. The town I see come quickly. Town spilling along crease of hills like scattering rocks. James-Face saying something as hooves pounding fast. We soon slow down and do not go into a town. Edge of crease, I see our house. Sun-up has not reached it. House always in shade. Is dark, as if we do not live there. Darkly hides among tall trees. Is James-Face a tall tree the first time I'm seeing him?

Individually the images in this quotation from *Arilla Sun Down*, which attempts to suggest a twelve-year-old remembering early childhood, work well, but there are too many of them, and the odd sentence structures which omit all sorts of key words sound pretentious. Few editors would allow the work of lesser writers to go to press in this way. In *The Gathering* difficulty comes from another kind of linguistic experimentation; there is a use here not of too many images but an excess of space jargon:

> "And danger," the figure toned. "You would not listen when Speaker ordered the Stay-in-time."
>
> "Speaker be in my dream. Triwaying on my own," toned Duster. "Be me Onewaying along, liking it."
>
> "Most Hellal IX," toned the figure. "Recall the Max of Sona. Out/Place-Out/Time. You must never be out of place."
>
> Duster hummed agreement. "And Mal be coming," Duster toned. "Remember be me falling flat in dark of Mal. Be following in It as It told me to. Me with some youngens in a dust place."

In the books from *Arilla Sun Down* to *The Gathering* language is often an endurance test, not a pleasure.

Yet the prose in *Zeely*, Virginia Hamilton's first novel, is uncluttered and luminous; sentences rise and fall with a poetry that leaves the reader admiring the clarity of thought and language, the vivid pictures — "The waning day she saw as clear as morning in the country; her father's words, bright as sunlight in the fields;" and "Long streets looked like spokes of a wheel connected to nothing and going nowhere."

> What they saw was no ordinary sight. They watched, spellbound, for nothing in the world could have prepared them for the sight of Miss Zeely Tayber.
>
> Zeely Tayber was more than six and a half feet tall, thin and deeply dark as a pole of Ceylon ebony. She wore a long smock that reached to her ankles. Her arms, hands and feet were bare, and her thin, oblong head didn't seem to fit quite right on her shoulders.
>
> She had very high cheekbones and her eyes seemed to turn inward on themselves . . .
>
> Zeely's long fingers looked exactly like bean pods left a long time in the sun.

This is as effective as anything Virginia Hamilton wrote in the books that followed: direct, simple description with the occasional image — the pole of Ceylon ebony, the fingers like bean pods — showing that the writer, even in this first novel, can use language with remarkable originality.

Zeely is a long short story for children; all Virginia Hamilton's subsequent work — with the exception of the two collections of Jahdu stories, *The Time-Ago Tales of Jahdu* and *Time-Ago Lost: More Tales of Jahdu* — has a teenage audience in mind. It is a pity she has not written more for younger readers, for *Zeely* has a straightforward, unpretentious narrative, clear-cut portraits of people, and in Geeder a sympathetic, highly imaginative central character. *Too* imaginative: that is the moral of the book. So "spellbound" is Geeder by Miss Tayber's looks and apparently odd behavior that she decides Zeely must be an African Queen, enslaved against her will by her brutal father to look after his hundreds of prize hogs; she goes around telling people this romantic nonsense, and eventually Zeely hears about it. There could, of course, be trouble at this point, but, in

Geeder, Zeely recognizes herself when young, and while gently telling the girl that in everyday life she should stick to the facts, she also encourages her to cling to and develop the gifts of her imagination. "I stopped making up tales a long time ago," she says, "and now I am myself;" but she adds, "You have a most fine way of dreaming. Hold on to that."

There is too much "dreaming" and not enough fact in *The House of Dies Drear*, which is a disappointment after *Zeely*. Its intentions are admirable, its background exciting. Virginia Hamilton's ancestors were slaves who fled from the South in the first half of the nineteenth century; "perhaps," she says (in an author's note in *The House of Dies Drear*), "with this book I have at last touched them the way they first touched me so long ago." The implausibility of much of the plot, however, stops the reader from being touched in the way she hoped. The Small family leave their home in North Carolina to live in Ohio (thus making the same journey as their black forefathers.) The house they rent had been used a hundred and fifty years previously as a staging post on one of the slaves' main escape routes; it belonged to Dies Drear, an abolitionist from a wealthy New England shipbuilding background. The house has many secret passages and false walls in which blacks on the run were hidden in times of trouble; the local community nowadays believes it is haunted. So far, so good: first-class material from which to fashion a story, though it is difficult to accept that Mrs. Small would agree to live in a haunted house. Unfortunately the author is not content with this. The neighbors, the Darrow family, try to frighten the Smalls into leaving the house because they think that hidden somewhere in it is a vast horde of treasure amassed by Dies Drear, and they want to get hold of it for themselves. The treasure does exist, in fact; it's hidden in an underground cave and has long ago been discovered by the caretaker of the house, Mr. Pluto, who himself lives in a cave. (The too obvious symbolic name Pluto, king of the underworld, is only one of many examples of clumsy thinking in this novel.) Mr. Pluto is old and ill, so his son, an actor, impersonates him, and together with the Small family he terrifies the Darrows into behaving themselves properly for the foreseeable future. This is all completely unbelievable: hidden treasure, greedy villains, ghosts and impersonations of ghosts belong to another genre than the one Virginia Hamilton probably wanted to explore; slave ancestry and color of skin are important and absorbing matters, but here they seem to be devalued into stage props, unlike, for example, similar material in Mildred Taylor's *Roll of Thunder, Hear My Cry*. The action is observed through the eyes of young Thomas Small, but he is not an interesting character out of whom events evolve; he is only a rather two-dimensional device for relaying the story to the reader. His parents are not much more than stereotypes, and the Plutos, father and son, are downright embarrassing. Yet the quality of the writing often impresses:

> The house of Dies Drear sat on an outcropping, much like a ledge, on the side of the hill. The face of the ledge was rock, from which gushed mineral springs. And these came together at the fertile land, making a narrow groove through it before emptying into the stream. Running down the face of the ledge, the springs coated the rock in their path with red and yellow rust.
>
> Thomas stared so long at the ledge and springs, his eyes began to play tricks on him. It seemed as if the rust moved along with the spring waters.
>
> "It's bleeding," he said softly.

The same problems exist in *The Planet of Junior Brown*. Here is a writer who certainly knows how to use words:

> A few trees struggled to grow in an atmosphere choked with automobile exhaust fumes. Junior found all of it beautiful — the stunted trees, the winter-brown plants and the old men and women. Out of the cheap retirement rooms of the side streets, the lonely old people rested awhile, like lost bundles on the cold, sunny benches.

All the characters are strange misfits. Junior himself is enormously fat, a dreamer who plays a piano that makes no sound; his mother is a neurotic, ailing snob, and his music teacher, who won't let him play the piano in her house and who imagines she has a relative of hers living in her wrecked sitting room, is insane. Mr. Pool, once a schoolteacher and now a janitor, spends most of his time in a darkened basement playing with a model of the solar system. Buddy Clark — intended as a sharp contrast to this bunch of grotesques — is the least convincing character of all. Homeless, parentless, he lives in a derelict house and is the leader, the "tomorrow Billy," of a group of runaway kids; they are his "planet." He keeps in touch with other similar "planets" and their leaders, and works at a newsstand to provide cash, food, and clothing for the kids he looks after. There is not a trace of delinquency in him, not a hint of squalor in the basement where he camps out; he is every inch a saint. This might perhaps be credible if he were an adult with a wide and rich experience of life, but he's a boy of thirteen. As it is impossible to believe in the reality of the characters, it is difficult to be sympathetic to their problems or care very much about what happens to them; so ultimately, therefore, the reader may well become bored. The pace of the narrative is slower than in the previous books, though not as slow as in *Arilla Sun Down* or *Justice and Her Brothers*, and the astronomical symbolism, besides being simplistic and intrusive, shows little real connection between the "planet" of homeless children and Mr. Pool's solar system with its extra planet called Junior Brown.

In *M.C. Higgins, the Great* there is credible plot and convincing characterization, which, combined with the author's writing skills and talents, lead to her most satisfying book since *Zeely*; it is indeed a much finer achievement than *Zeely* as its range and depth are far greater. Landscape plays a more important role in this novel than any other of Virginia Hamilton's: we are in a remote mountainous part of Ohio; it is a landscape that has moulded the character of the few people who live there, including the protagonists of the book, M.C. and his parents, Jones and Banina Higgins. They are the rural poor — Banina cleans houses and Jones works occasionally at a steel mill in the nearest city — but they love the mountains, are rarely happy when they are elsewhere. Hanging over their lives, however, is a terrible threat: mining work in the area has created a huge and ugly spoil-heap which is so unsafe that a lengthy period of rain might cause it to shift and destroy not only the family's house, but also their lives. It is impossible, when reading this book, not to be reminded of the tragedy that occurred in 1967 at Aberfan in Wales, when a heap of slurry crashed down a mountain-side and killed some eighty children who were in a school at the time: they were buried alive. Jones refuses to believe that the danger is real; even discussing the subject annoys him. But M.C. knows they will have to move. The idea of moving is effectively combined with M.C.'s knowledge that he is growing up — the idyllic mountain country becomes synonymous with childhood, and at thirteen he knows, regretfully, that he has to leave childhood behind. The other features of the story are simple and few. M.C. has a brief friendship with a girl he meets — his first experience of adolescence rather than childhood, and it is a transitory, bitter-sweet relationship, not at all like the certainties of his earlier life. The only event, apart from this, is his encounter with a man who is making tape recordings of the songs of the people who live in the area: M.C. hopes this will lead to his mother becoming famous and earning enough money for the family to move away. Such a hope is childish, of course, and the outcome is predictably a disappointment for him. The ending of the book shows him building a wall at the back of the house to keep the spoil out should it cascade down the mountain. He has abandoned the idea of leaving, perhaps leaving the family; the last few pages show him for once contented and peaceful with his parents, brothers, sisters, and friends —

There began to take shape a long, firm kind of mound. The children fed it. M.C. shoveled and Ben packed it. In the immense quiet of Sarah's Mountain late in the day, they formed a wall. And it was rising.

— but it is no happy ending; the reader is left with the ominous sensation that tragedy will inevitably occur, just as it would be tragic not to move out of childhood. No wall, however massive and strong, can possibly hold back the force of thousands of tons of slurry. Or the arrival of adulthood. The wall's symbolic intention is similar to the use Jan Mark makes of the hole Matthew digs in *Under the Autumn Garden*.

All the characters in this book, even the mysterious interbred Killburns with their six fingers on each hand and reputations as witches, are complex, rounded, living people, and the different layers of love and caring, anger and irritation, in the Higgins family are totally convincing. Jones is a delightful portrait of a man who is at the age when he begins to regret the loss of his youthfulness; his eldest child, M.C., he regards with a mixture of affection and threat: M.C. is starting to compete with him on almost equal terms. This is neatly implied in the way Virginia Hamilton describes him:

> Jones was a powerfully built man. He wasn't tall, but he had a broad chest and lean but wide, muscular shoulders. He was narrow through the hips just as M.C. was, and his legs were long with muscles grown lengthwise. His toes were splayed with the bridge flattened wide, as were M.C.'s, the way a swimmer's feet will look. Jones was a swimmer. But somehow, his fine, physical equipment had never quite come together. As a man, he wasn't as good a swimmer as M.C. was right now.
>
> What will I be, at his age? M.C. wondered.
> *Be on this mountain*, his mind spoke for Jones.
> No, M.C. thought.

The relationship between M.C. and Jones is one of the most impressive father-son relationships in contemporary children's literature. We see a great deal, too, of the life M.C. shares with his mother, and also glimpses of his parents' marriage (a stable, loving, committed marriage), but if these are less striking, and Banina less frequently observed than Jones, that is because everything is viewed through M.C.'s eyes: he is at an age when his father is more important to him than his mother is. Again, it is part of the contrast between childhood and adolescence that is such a major theme in this novel — Banina represents for M.C. the certainties and happiness of childhood; Jones, he is aware, is not unlike what he will be himself because Jones is a man; his father, in this sense, represents the future as well as the past.

Landscape, as I said, is ever present, and so is the weather; Virginia Hamilton's prose brings this background vividly alive:

> Now he listened. He saw the sky grow heavy with mist as he watched. It turned gray and, finally, dark. He heard sound coming. Rain, like hundreds of mice running through corn. He watched it come over the mountain and down the slope in a straight line.
>
> M.C. hadn't bothered to move from the step. He had already felt the rain, seen it without seeing.
>
> Wind hit Jones first. It ran before the rain. Jones didn't want his clothes soaked, so he stepped onto the porch while rain came full of mist, but hard all the same.
>
> They watched it. The rain marched down Sarah's and on across, turning hill after hill the same shade of silver mist clear to the river. Then it was gone from the mountain. As it had come, clawing through cornstalk, it vanished with the same familiar sound.

M.C. Higgins, the Great is a very fine achievement and thoroughly deserved the awards of the Newbery Medal and the National Book Award it received in 1974.

Arilla Sun Down suffers from the old fault of some improbable characters, and a narrative pace that is far too slow. Events and people are smothered by the words:

lengthy asides, interesting in themselves, distract the reader's attention, and descriptive passages lose their effect in language that is at times unnecessarily complex. Almost all the characters in Virginia Hamilton's novels are black, but this is not a point worth discussing any more than it is worthwhile to speculate on why Alan Garner's characters are all white — except in *Arilla Sun Down*, where race *is* an issue. The Adams family are part black, part Indian; there is conflict between the women (Arilla and her mother) who think this is a matter of little importance, and the men (her father and her brother, Jack Sun Run) who are aware — or think they are aware — of the sad implications of their lost Indian heritage. This theme should, perhaps, have provided the book's main interest, but it gets lost under the weight of surface detail; it is only at the end that it seems more important than it has appeared to be, when Arilla chooses her Indian name — Sun Down. The plot moves from one lengthy static scene to another. The evening at the skating rink, Arilla's birthday party (odd — and oddly repetitive — that in most of Virginia Hamilton's novels the central character has a birthday party), the fourth of July celebrations when Jack Sun Run lassos two men he thinks have been rude to him, the snowstorm — all are big set-pieces, elaborate and leisurely like a carefully composed photograph: one is never aware of the excitement of a continuously developing narrative. The telling of the story is in two styles — Arilla's memories of early childhood, fragmentary, confusing, and written, as I said earlier, with most of the key words left out; and Arilla speaking quite normally as a twelve-year-old girl. The two styles do not harmonize well, for each shows up the other's inadequacies.

Jack Sun Run is quite unbelievable. At fifteen his skill with horses, his courage and judgment, are those of an experienced and mature man; as with Buddy Clark in *The Planet of Junior Brown* we are not really seeing a teenager at all, but an adult. (Even M.C. Higgins seems older than thirteen; his thinking processes and feelings are often those of a boy of at least fifteen.) The way Jack Sun Run is constantly presented as some kind of god is wearisome:

> And here is my brother, Sun, wearing nothing above the waist; wearing cowhide leggings and Wellington boots, with his bare arms, shoulders and back shining like antique gold from his sweat.

Or this:

> Mom says Sun has an "aura" about him. It's true, because about every sidewalk sale they have in the spring, when they close off the streets downtown, folks will stop what they are doing to watch Sun parading Jeremiah. Sitting so still in his skins, like he is taking a long ride through a painted desert — it will seem like the day is holding its breath until he is finished showing off. Anytime something seems to be missing, or some event is going to turn into a real bore, all of a sudden here comes Jack Sun Run and the day just sucks in its breath, then breezes in place around him.

Maybe it is the first person narration that is the major fault. Though Arilla perceives her parents' placement of themselves in the town's social strata quite clearly, her eyes are, for the most part, too hazy to see character and event as having independent lives of their own.

Justice and Her Brothers, Dustland, and *The Gathering* form a trilogy called *The Justice Cycle.* These three books are works of science fiction, and the author seems as happy in this genre as she is in the realistic stories that had previously been her preoccupation. She says she feels less involved with her own heritage now and more interested in survivors. "Will the few who survive the cataclysm do so because they are genetically different?" she asks (in an author's note in *Dustland*). "Is it possible that telepathy, prophecy, and genius are genetic mutations? Could the striking talents of a few be the means of survival for many?" But the central character of the trilogy, the eleven-year-old girl, Justice, is involved to a great degree with her family, her roots, with the difficult and inharmonious relationship between her twin brothers, Thomas and Levi — there are several resonances here with other novels about twins, Katherine Paterson's *Jacob Have I Loved*, for example, and Penelope Farmer's *Year King* — and she uses the knowledge and power gained from the adventures she and her brothers have in the future to help heal the wounds of her family in the present.

The first hundred pages of *Justice and Her Brothers* give few hints to the reader that the story will ultimately be concerned with children who have extraordinary powers of extra-sensory perception, who have the ability to read minds and project themselves into the future. This first part of the book has an almost snail's pace narrative; place, weather, family, friends are portrayed in great detail, and the story seems to be revolving around only one event, the Great Snake Race that Thomas has organized for the kids of the neighborhood. It comes as quite a surprise when the novel departs from the realistic tale we have assumed it is going to be, but the clues are there; the science fiction genre to which it belongs isn't an afterthought, tacked on, as it were, because the author felt her realistic story was not going to function properly. *Justice and Her Brothers* is concerned with the development of the children's amazing abilities, not with the use to which those abilities are put — that is the function of *Dustland* and *The Gathering*. It is also concerned with the pattern of relationships in the Douglass family and the delineation of character. This, I think, is in some ways a mistake from a structural point of view; it leaves no room in the second and third books for development of character, for change. We know that whatever happens, Thomas is always the odd one out; the one who for entirely selfish reasons puts the other two and their friend, Dorian Jefferson, into some kind of danger; who, whatever happens, dislikes Justice because she has more power than he has. Levi is always the one who suffers most from Thomas's neurotic behavior; Dorian — whose character is never fully explored — invariably manages to heal him. Thomas's motives are well summed up in this comment from *Justice and Her Brothers*:

> Thomas couldn't remember a time when he had liked Justice much. Now, admitting her greater power, he knew they would never be close. Yet he did care about Levi. He had abused his brother. He had toyed with him, as a cat with a mouse. For all his cruelty — and Thomas knew he had been terribly cruel to Levi — there was still a part of him that would protect his brother. Regretfully, he would one day abandon Levi to his sister and Dorian, if Justice was to be believed. To think of leaving his identical behind, even in some far-off future, brought him a depth of sorrow no singleton would understand.

Dustland and *The Gathering* are different from *Justice and Her Brothers*, less reflective, less analytical, more concerned with the creation of imaginary worlds. In *Dustland*, Virginia Hamilton's vision of the future on planet Earth, civilization destroyed apart from a few extraordinary creatures who have managed to survive the holocaust, the surface of the world totally barren, a desert of dust so thick that even the air chokes the sunlight, is a powerful and bleak picture of what just possibly could happen. Her gift for language, however, for the first time falters occasionally; the vague adverb or adjective is used when more precise descriptive words are needed: "They had passed through Dustland's unbelievable dawn an hour ago." No comment other than the dawn being "unbelievable" is unsatisfactory. It is a small fault, but it is also present in *The Gathering*; and in this final part of the trilogy language is sometimes used in a solemn, quasi-biblical way — "What was there they saw, yet did not see" — as if an attempt is being made to suggest a significance that the author has not otherwise justified. In *The Gathering*, the children discover the domed city-state of Sona, one of a dozen or so attempts to replant Earth with new forms of life. There is quite a large collection of the usual bug-eyed monsters and intergalactic hardware one finds in a great deal of space fiction; Virginia

Hamilton's creatures and machines are no more and no less convincing than those of several other writers. (One is reminded a little of the domed cities and strange beings in John Christopher's *City of Gold and Lead*.) Too much emphasis is given in *The Gathering* to these imaginings of future life: the result is that this novel has not enough narration, too much explanation. *Dustland*, therefore, is, of the three books, the most enjoyable to read.

Sweet Whispers, Brother Rush, though the first few chapters are slow, has a narrative that, for the most part, sets enough pace to hold the reader's attention, and the writing does not suffer from the obscurity that mars some of its predecessors; the result is Virginia Hamilton's best novel since *M.C. Higgins, the Great*. It is the story of fifteen-year-old Tree, left at home to look after her retarded elder brother, Dabney, while her mother is away in another town, working. Absence of mothers is a recurring theme in Virginia Hamilton's work — Justice's mother attends classes at college, Arilla's mother teaches long hours at a dance studio. In *Sweet Whispers, Brother Rush*, the father is also missing — Ken deserted his wife and kids long ago. Tree is a very deprived child; when her mother's boy friend, Silversmith, takes her to a cafeteria, "She'd never seen such good-looking Jello, green and yellow and red and orange." When Silversmith says they'll take her out dancing, she says, " 'Me?' Tree was astonished. 'Dancin? Me?' " Parental deprivation, however, is much worse for her than the absence of the ordinary pleasures of life. Her complex relationship with her mother, Vy, is the center of the book — a relationship that is at times warm and loving, but Tree is also angry and embittered by her mother's selfishness and the cold way she treats Dabney. Tree's love for her brother is a crucial element in the story. Elder brothers being important to younger sisters is another recurring theme of Virginia Hamilton's — it has a large place in the *Justice* trilogy and in *Arilla Sun Down*: but in *Sweet Whispers, Brother Rush* it is different in that it is without antagonism. Most of all, Tree is deprived of history — she knows nothing of her mother's background, her father, her uncles. It has been hidden from her, as it is from the reader for half of the book, and it is a tragic history — the uncles died young from porphyria, and the youngest (called Brother) let himself be killed in a car crash because he knew that he, too, was dying from the same disease. Dabney also dies of porphyria. It is a depressing, sad story; its message is, in the words of Silversmith,

> . . . . you can't run away from what you've lost or what you love, either. I carried the love for my dad with me. I couldn't get away from it. I couldn't lose the loss of my mother.

But it ends hopefully — Silversmith is a good man, a substitute father for Tree; it seems probable that he will marry Vy, and his son Don begins to date Tree.

Tree discovers the family history through the appearance of the ghost of her Uncle Brother, which is an unsatisfactory device — in such a realistic novel as this, the use of the supernatural seems like a cheap short cut to give Tree knowledge: the author should have found a more convincing way of imparting information, particularly as the information, once given, leaves the ghost without any proper function in the story. Nevertheless, the need children have for a sense of the past, especially the past of their own families, is made convincing as Tree is so believable:

> How come I never think to ask anything? She answered her own question.
> If you never told there's some answers, how you gone know the questions?

The prose style, though not easy, and on a few occasions pretentious — "It entered her mind, where her thoughts were shaken up and rearranged in preparation for that which was beyond her knowledge" — is on the whole excellent, uncluttered and musical, full of sharp, original observations:

> "We will leave the diagnosing to the specialist," the nurse said. She had read a minute from the folder.

Now she closed it and held it against her. She wasn't being unkind. But she was crisp, like a cold head of lettuce.

It would seem that in *Sweet Whispers, Brother Rush*, Virginia Hamilton has, despite saying in *Dustland* that she is now more interested in survivors, returned to the idea of roots and heritage; in doing so she has produced a much more readable novel than any of those in the *Justice* trilogy.

The judgments in this essay may sound harsh, but Virginia Hamilton is too gifted an author to be assessed other than by the most exacting standards. Her achievement is not unlike that of Alan Garner: both are writers talented far more than most, but the books they have written — with a few exceptions — contain too many serious flaws.

References

VIRGINIA HAMILTON
Zeely Macmillan, New York, 1967
The House of Dies Drear Macmillan, New York, 1968
The Time-Ago Tales of Jahdu Macmillan, New York, 1969
The Planet of Junior Brown Macmillan, New York, 1971
Time-Ago Lost: More Tales of Jahdu Macmillan, New York, 1973
M.C. Higgins, the Great Macmillan, New York, 1974; Hamish Hamilton 1975
Arilla Sun Down Greenwillow 1976; Hamish Hamilton 1977
Justice and Her Brothers Greenwillow 1978; Hamish Hamilton 1979
Dustland Greenwillow 1980; Julia Macrae Books 1980
The Gathering Greenwillow 1981
Sweet Whispers, Brother Rush Philomel 1982

JOHN CHRISTOPHER
The City of Gold and Lead Hamish Hamilton 1967; Macmillan, New York, 1967

PENELOPE FARMER
Year King Chatto 1977; Atheneum 1977

JAN MARK
  Under the Autumn Garden Kestrel 1977; Crowell 1979
KATHERINE PATERSON
  Jacob Have I Loved Crowell 1980; Gollancz 1981
MILDRED TAYLOR
  Roll of Thunder, Hear My Cry Dial 1976; Gollancz 1977

Index

Permission Acknowledgments